WIFE FIVE

A Play by

Steve Hayes
And
Michelle Morgan

Wife Five
A Play by Steve Hayes And Michelle Morgan
© Steve Hayes/Michelle Morgan, 2013. All Rights Reserved.
No part of this book may be reproduced in any form or by any means, electronic, mechanical, digital, photocopying or recording, except for the inclusion in a review, without permission in writing from the publisher.

Published in the USA by:
BearManor Media
P O Box 71426
Albany, Georgia 31708
www.bearmanormedia.com

ISBN: 978-1-59393-740-9
Printed in the United States of America
Book design by Robbie Adkins

Steve Hayes's dedication:
"To Robbin, with love."

Michelle Morgan's dedication:
"To Paul, Wendy, and Angelina, with love."

WIFE FIVE

The action of the play takes place in a Malibu beach home, apart from the first and last scenes, which take place in a coroner's laboratory.

The time is the present.

ACT ONE
Scene 1

Curtain rises. Lights come up. Center-stage is the corner of a laboratory made up of a partial rear and side wall. In the rear wall is a door marked: "Forensics." On the side wall hangs an X-ray viewer. Below it is a counter covered with medical paraphernalia. Potted cacti sit atop a filing cabinet, trying to bring the outdoors to this white antiseptic environment, while jazz music plays softly on a CD player.

DR. ABIGAIL "ABBY" EDMONDS, thirty, a blonde, elegant woman wearing a white lab coat over her blouse and jeans, sits at the counter studying a slide under a microscope. She records her findings in a notebook.

A MALE LAB ASSISTANT (earrings, nose-rings, tattoos) wheels in a table on which a "corpse" lies covered with a sheet. Poking out from under the sheet is a bare foot with an ID tag tied to its big toe.

But that isn't what catches our attention. WHAT DOES CATCH OUR ATTENTION is that the "corpse" apparently died with an erection—an erection that, if we're to believe the size of the "tent" it makes above the groin area, is nothing short of, well... spectacular!

LAB ASSISTANT: Sorry to spoil your weekend, doc, but I've got a last-minute customer for you.

ABBY (not looking up): Be with you in a sec.

LAB ASSISTANT: The coroner says he wants you to do an autopsy, ASAP.

ABBY (writing on notepad): Ritchie, why do you insist on calling our boss the coroner? He has a name, you know.

LAB ASSISTANT: Yeah, like, anyone can pronounce it.

ABBY: What's so hard about Tananteguchi? Tan-an-te-guchi? If you want a name that really swivels your tongue, try pronouncing his predecessor's: Suvorov Kosciusensko.

> Finished writing, she turns and looks at the Lab Assistant and then at the "corpse"—her eyebrows arching abruptly as, for the first time, she sees the apparent huge erection.

(softly awed): Holy shit.

LAB ASSISTANT (grins): Gives new meaning to the phrase "died in the saddle," wouldn't you say? (saluting goodbye) Happy Labor Day, doc.

> Laughing, he exits left. Abby, eyeing the "tent" with a mixture of awe and disbelief, goes to the table and reads the ID tag, which is tied to his toe.

ABBY: Well, Mr. Hoag, I imagine your death has caused your wife or girlfriend more than the usual amount of dismay. I've never been one to place too much importance on size over performance, but I can't help admiring a Guinness world record when I see one.

> She starts to lift the sheet.

Just then, the "corpse" SITS UP and in the same motion whips aside the sheet, (making Abby jump back with a startled gasp) and we see what is really causing the erection: a potted prickly pear cactus held by a man wearing a T-shirt, shorts, and one flip-flop—the other is on the table.

Say hello to HARRY SPAIN, a lean, suntanned beach-rat writer who is in his late forties but looks and acts younger, mainly as a result of hanging out with people much younger than himself.

ABBY (anger and shock mixed): Jesus fucking Christ, Harry!

She angrily punches him on the arm, while all the time Harry keeps laughing like an idiot as he removes the toe-tag, puts his flip-flop back on, and climbs down off the table.

HARRY: Gotcha, didn't I?

ABBY: GOT ME? Are you nuts? Don't you know you could've given me a heart attack? (still punching him) It's a wonder I didn't keel over right on the spot! (worn out, she stops punching) Damn you, Harry, when the hell are you gonna grow up?

HARRY (weak from laughter): Hopefully, never.

ABBY: Well, in future, confine your schoolyard pranks to all your bimbos —whom I'm sure just giggle themselves to death over it.

HARRY (playfully): Meeoww.

ABBY: Harry, before I grab a scalpel and make like Jack-the-Ripper, tell me you're not suggesting I'm jealous of those nauseously erotic young women who parade their silicon-enhanced bodies in front of your beach house?

HARRY (backing up alarmed): Hey, cool it, Slim. I'm just kidding, okay?

ABBY: Well, "kid" somewhere else. What're you doing here, anyway?

HARRY: I just came from a writers' meeting at the Soap Factory and thought I'd brighten up your day by buying you lunch.

ABBY: At four (checks her watch) forty-five in the afternoon?

HARRY: (unfazed): Dinner, then? How about it? We'll drive up to Paradise Cove, nibble on some shrimp, sip chilled Chardonnay, and then kick back and hold hands while we watch the sun go down. (suddenly realizing he's still holding the potted cactus) Oh, this puppy's for you.

ABBY (ignores the cactus): Harry—

HARRY (talking incessantly): Genus Opuntia. Member of the Family Cactaceae. Also known in Spanish as Nopales—

ABBY: Harry, please—

HARRY: Its pads and fruit are not only edible but you can also make syrup or jelly or even candy from them. Bet you didn't know that, did you?

ABBY (not angrily but firmly): Harry, shut up. (as he obeys) Thank you.

HARRY: You're welcome.

ABBY: Now, do you mind telling me why you're really here?

HARRY: I told you: to take you to dinner.

ABBY: Harry—

HARRY: It's the truth. As I was driving down Wilshire toward PCH, I suddenly thought, hey, this isn't far from where Abby works and—

ABBY: That's enough! (as he subsides) Harry, I don't believe you for one second. Oh, you may have been driving along Wilshire, and you might have remembered I work nearby, but for you to stop and take the time to buy me a cactus and then not only find a parking space but know that you're going to have to pay for the privilege of parking—something you hate more than... than... God I don't know... anything—well, the motive has to be more than just dinner.

HARRY: You're right. I do hate paying for parking and I'm the first to admit it. But as to why I'm here and why I bought you the cactus, well, for once, you're way off base. 'Cause, so help me, Slim, I just thought it would be nice to see you and spend some time together over a drink or something. (pauses, then darkly) In case you've forgotten, madam, I am known in the biz as the "Writer-who-always-speaks-with-straight-tongue."

ABBY: That's true—to everyone but me, it seems. Why is that, Harry? What is it about me that brings out your devious side?

HARRY: Madam, I'm hurt beyond belief.

ABBY: Yeah, right. (off his look of sincerity) Okay, okay, just this once I'll buy into your straight-arrow routine.

HARRY: Wonderful! Grab your coat!

ABBY: Sorry, I already have a dinner date.

HARRY: Can't you postpone it?

ABBY: No-I-can't-postpone-it. And I wouldn't, even if I could.

HARRY: Why not? Hell, we haven't had dinner together for... ages.

ABBY: All the more reason I should keep this engagement. Not that I need a reason, since the man I'm dining with is my boyfriend.

HARRY (irked): Ugh, does that mean you're still seeing Brent?

ABBY: It's "Brett", as if you didn't know. And yes, I'm still seeing him. That's what people do, you know, when they're dating regularly: keep seeing each other.

HARRY: Not if they've got any brains.

> Abby shoots him a dangerous look, moves to the counter, and picks up a wicked-looking scalpel. Harry immediately backs up, potted cactus held before him protectively.

HARRY: Okay, so Mr. Architect's still hanging around. Can't blame him, I guess. (sets cactus on the table) You're a keeper, no doubt about that—

ABBY: How would you know? If I remember correctly, <u>you</u> didn't keep me.

HARRY: Hey, that's below the belt—

ABBY: In fact, you seemed intent on chasing me as far away as humanly possible.

HARRY (avoiding eye contact): Everybody's entitled to one mistake.

ABBY: Oh, is that what you call it when you get divorced: a mistake?

HARRY: <u>I</u> didn't <u>get</u> divorced, you did. Remember?

ABBY: And why did I do that, I wonder? Could it be because I grew tired of being separated from the man I once loved. A man who, I might add, not only refused to discuss reconciliation but seemed fanatically opposed to even considering any form of it.

HARRY: That's not true. Like I kept telling you, I just needed more time.

ABBY: So you did. And of course it never occurred to you—locked up in that convoluted little world of imagination you live in—that after two years of denial on my part—denial that our marriage had indeed come to an unhappy conclusion—I finally forced myself to call a lawyer and make legal what you, I, and every horny bimbo cavorting on Malibu Beach—maybe even the entire West Coast for all I know—knew from the start: that we as a married couple were over. Done with. Finis. Caput.

HARRY: "Cavorting"?

ABBY (had it): Goodbye, Harry.

HARRY (amused): "Cavorting"?

ABBY: Yes, cavorting. If the term offends you, forgive me. Not being a brilliant soap writer such as yourself—

HARRY: No, no, I was just picturing certain bikini-clad buds of mine that I was playing volleyball with yesterday and, by God, you're absolutely right: cavorting is the perfect description. I commend you on it.

ABBY: I'm _so_ glad you're pleased. Nice to be appreciated—even when it's by your ex-husband. (indicates door) Now, please, do me a favor and commend me somewhere else. Or in your words, do the old El Scrammo.

HARRY (moving off): Yeah, sure. See ya tomorrow, then.

ABBY: Tomorrow?

HARRY: It's Saturday, remember?

ABBY: Oh... yes... well, be that as it may I don't think—

HARRY: Everybody's gonna be there. All day. I'm barbecuing.

ABBY: Yeah, but this is a long weekend, and I'm sure Brett and I have plans—

HARRY (pouncing): Has Brent told you he has plans?

ABBY: Brett! And no, but...

HARRY: Ah-hah! So, he hasn't told you he's doing anything, and by now, since it's already Friday afternoon and almost the beginning of the long holiday weekend, you're beginning to wonder if he is actually going to call, or if he'll spend the weekend with his blue prints and pencils instead of you. Man this must be really pissing you off.

ABBY: I didn't say that—

HARRY: You didn't have to. We were married, remember? I know you like an old Faulkner novel. You hate it when people leave things to the last minute. You've told me, God knows how many times, it upsets your mental rhythms, your sense of order, your desire to keep everything neat and tidy in that perfect little brain of yours—

ABBY: My brain is not little, thank you—

HARRY: Sorry, slip of the tongue. No, your brain is more than adequate, I'd say. Much more than adequate. In fact your brain is one of those brains that undoubtedly deserves to be on display in the Smithsonian—up there with the brains of Einstein, Newton, Tolstoy—

> Abby, despite being irked, can't help but laugh—which she knows is the worst thing she can do because it only encourages him.

HARRY (without pausing):—and, just so I can't be accused of chauvinism, let me include: Helen Keller, Madame Curie, Marilyn Monroe—

ABBY (wearily): Oh, Harry, please, for Pete's sake shut up, will you, and remove yourself from my lab.

HARRY: Soon as you answer me about tomorrow. In fact I got a great idea. Bring Brent along. Isn't it about time we all met your future hubby?

ABBY (instinct telling her this is a big mistake): I don't know, Harry. I'm not sure I'm ready to—

HARRY: <u>You're</u> not or Brent's not? (as she wags the scalpel at him) Okay, Brett—Brett's not? Which is it? (as she hesitates) What's the matter? Here's the perfect chance to show all of us that lover-boy not only isn't the jerk I think he is but is, in fact, a mixture of Johnny Depp, George Clooney, and Brad Pitt all rolled into one.

ABBY (defensively): Looks aren't everything, you know.

HARRY: Okay, so now we know Brett's not the "hunk of the week."

ABBY: I never said that. God, why do you always put words into my mouth?

HARRY: Aww, I'm just teasing. It doesn't matter what he looks like, Slim. Knowing you I'm sure he's got brains instead. Bring the dude anyway. We're all open-minded. And I promise not to judge.

ABBY (a sore spot): Why don't you just shut the fuck up, Harry? Just close your mouth for once, okay?

HARRY: Uh-oh, this relationship isn't good for you.

ABBY: What're you talking about?

HARRY: You never said "fuck" when you were married to me. In fact, you hardly cussed at all. Now in a short period of time you've said it twice.

ABBY: Oh I cussed. Just not in front of you—which, considering how crazy you drove me all the time, surely makes me a candidate for the Medal of Honor.

HARRY: Medal of Honor's for bravery. You mean an Academy Award.

ABBY (looks at him as if he isn't real): What I really mean is, I should've shot you at least a hundred times.

HARRY: Now you're getting hysterical.

ABBY: Harry, I'm gonna count to five. If you're not gone by then, I'm going to perform open heart surgery on you—without anesthetic!

HARRY: I'm going, I'm going. Just tell me if you and Brett the Bridge-builder are coming Saturday or not, so I can tell everyone.

ABBY: By "everyone" I presume you mean the regulars?

HARRY: Who else? Like you've told me a zillion times, I don't have any friends. I just got four ex-wives and a housekeeper who hates my guts.

ABBY: I never said that. (off his look) Did I? (off his imperious nod) Well, if I did, that was rude of me, and I sincerely apologize.

HARRY: Apology accepted. So... you'll bring him?

ABBY: I don't know. (cornered) God, Harry, why do you always do this to me?

HARRY: Do what?

ABBY: Get me so mixed up, I never know whether I'm coming or going?

HARRY: Fat chance. In all the years I've known you, Slim, there's never been a moment when you didn't know <u>exactly</u> where you were at. And I do mean exactly. It's not only something I learned to expect but something I've always admired about you.

ABBY (surprised): You have?

HARRY: Absolutely. (grins) Now, all I'm asking for is some kind of yes or no. Surely that's not too much for you and that Smithsonian brain of yours to handle?

ABBY (could strangle him): All right, all right, tell you what - I'll ask Brett if he'd like to come. If he wants to, fine. But if he doesn't—

HARRY: Then you'll come alone. I'm cool with that. (kisses her on the cheek) See ya, Slim.

> He's gone, ducking out like a thief in the night. Abby looks after him, shaking her head, angry at first but then, like everyone Harry comes in contact with, forgiving him, a smile indicating she's now amused by his actions. Sighing, she picks up his gift and fondly sets it among the other cacti.

ABBY (to new cactus): Harry, Harry, Harry, why the hell did you ever come into my life?

> Lights dim.

Scene 2

A Malibu beach house. One big room with windows stretching across the entire upstage wall, overlooking a spectacular view of the beach and the ocean. The furniture is colorful and beachy. Potted palms and hanging plants are everywhere. There's a wet bar on the left and a door leading to the kitchen on the right. Another door, near the wet bar, opens out onto a sundeck. A spiral staircase leads up to the first-floor bedrooms, which we can't see.

A tripod telescope, for ogling girls on the beach, sits by the window.

In the upstage right corner is a drafting table, which can be raised or lowered, depending on if you want to work sitting or standing. Presently, it's raised and covered with writing materials. A desk with drawers and a chair sit next to it. A computer and a printer rest atop the desk, along with an old-fashioned telephone.

One of Harry's ex-wives, JESSICA DUNCAN and the housekeeper, MATTIE FYNE, are standing together in a yoga Tree pose, next to the right wall. Jessica is thirty-three, a willowy, tanned beauty-queen-type who has striking blonde hair and is wearing comfortable but flattering clothes. Mattie, in her fifties, is a matronly woman who does not dress to impress—in fact she looks as though she hasn't been near a clothes shop in years.

MATTIE (already in conversation): Help me out here... You mean to tell me that you've got this great hunk of a guy who loves you and spoils you to death and, oh-by-the-way wants to marry you, and your only problem is you can't make up your mind if he's: Mr. Right?

JESSICA: I know it sounds crazy, but—

MATTIE: Oh, it's crazy all right.

> Jessica lowers her leg and sits down cross-legged, mulling things over.

MATTIE: It's about as crazy as it gets, if you wanna know the truth. I could understand if you didn't love him but—

> She lowers herself and sits beside Jessica, adding:

You <u>do</u> love him, don't you?

JESSICA (hesitates then nods): Yes.

MATTIE: Oh my, oh my.

JESSICA: What? What?

MATTIE: You hesitated.

JESSICA: I did not.

MATTIE: Yes, you did. I said "you do love him, don't you?" And instead of saying yes right off the bat, you hesitated. Only for a second, mind, but—

JESSICA: Okay, so I hesitated. So what?

MATTIE: So what? Girl, hesitation is the kiss of death where true love's concerned. Everyone knows that.

JESSICA: Oh, for God's sake, Mattie, quit being so goddamned dramatic.

> Rising, she goes to the window and stares out at the beach. Mattie rises, and she follows her like a terrier nipping at her heels.

MATTIE: I'm not being dramatic and you know it.

JESSICA: I don't know anything and nor do you, so get off my case. If I want to be analyzed, I'll rent a couch.

MATTIE: Hey, don't get pissy with me. It ain't my fault you're about to blow off the catch of the century.

JESSICA: Who's blowing him off? Just 'cause I'm vacillating a little doesn't mean I'm not going to marry Richard.

MATTIE: What does it mean, then?

JESSICA: I don't know. Probably nothing! Getting married a second time's a big deal, and I'm just a little stressed out, that's all.

MATTIE: Now why didn't I think of that?

JESSICA: Save the sarcasm. You don't know everything, you know.

MATTIE: Never said I did. But if you want my advice—

JESSICA: I don't. So, let's just drop the subject, okay? I came out here to get some sun and collect my thoughts. (walking away) Advice is the last thing I—

> She pauses, halfway to the sundeck door, turns as she "feels" Mattie's eyes burning a hole in her back and looks questioningly at the housekeeper, who has the air of a wise old sage. Long beat as neither speaks, then Mattie can't hold it back any longer:

MATTIE: You need to start dating. (as Jessica looks pissed) I knew deep down you wanted to know, so I told you.

JESSICA: Dating? DATING?! <u>That's</u> your frigging advice?

MATTIE: Sure. For as long as I've known you, Jessica, you've always been too busy studying or working to really play the field. You need to get it all outta your system and then settle down.

JESSICA: Harry'll be pleased to hear that.

MATTIE: What's Harry got to do with it? He was just a blip on your radar screen.

JESSICA: He'll be even _more_ pleased to hear that.

MATTIE: What I mean is, now's your chance. Get out there in the trenches and check out how others stack up against your Richard.

JESSICA: Are you insane? I'm supposed to be getting married in like thirty-seven days and you want me to start dating? That's crazy. Richard would never put up with it, and I wouldn't respect him if he did.

MATTIE: So, don't tell him. I mean, it ain't like you're cheating.

JESSICA: It's not?

MATTIE: Course not. Not if you give it one of them fancy medical terms you're always throwing around. Then it's just a whadyacallit... a human study. You know a psychologist's attempt to find the perfect specimen.

JESSICA (covering her ears): I'm not listening to this.

MATTIE: What's the big deal? You do studies all the time, so Richard won't be suspicious even if he does catch you kissing another guy.

JESSICA (worn out): Please... go away. You're giving me a migraine.

MATTIE: Listen, you have the perfect setup. You've got guys running in and out of your office all day long—

JESSICA (incredulous): You want me to date my patients? Guys who're paying me to cure their sexual hang-ups? Oh yeah, I can't wait to choose Mr. Right from one of those penis-pushers.

MATTIE: Okay, so maybe that's not such a good idea. (brightens) Okay, I bet there's plenty other eligible hunks in your building. And what about all those dinner parties and weekend lectures and seminars you keep getting invited to? There's gotta be a Mr. Right somewhere in there.

JESSICA: And you know this to be true because, why? You've attended so many?

MATTIE (rolls her eyes): Zillions.

JESSICA: Well, I have, and believe me, Mattie, every one I go to only makes Richard look more like the catch of the century.

MATTIE: Then, there's your answer.

JESSICA: Answer?

MATTIE: Marry Richard, like I've been telling you all along—

> Jessica is open-mouthed as Mattie breaks off when the front door opens. Both women turn towards it, and in walks GLORIA DE WITT—another of Harry's ex-wives—an attractive, tall woman with beautiful short blonde hair, and she's wearing Gucci sunglasses. Though Gloria at thirty-eight is older than Jessica or Abby and doesn't facially resemble either of them, her coloring and figure are the same, and you'd be forgiven if you thought all three were sisters.

GLORIA: Hi, guys. (sees them swap looks) What's going on? Did I miss something? Details. I want details. Give, give, give.

MATTIE (needling): Ms. Vaginator, here—

JESSICA: That's vacillator, you bean-brain!

MATTIE: Miss <u>Vacillator</u> can't decide if she wants to marry Richard or someone else entirely.

JESSICA: That's not true! Dammit, Mattie, why don't you keep your nose out of my business?

MATTIE: You come to my house, and everything you say is my business.

GLORIA: Mattie, much as I adore you, this is not your house.

MATTIE: I'll remember that, Gloria, next time you want me to fix you a café latte or listen to your problems at one o'clock in the morning.

    Stung, she starts toward the kitchen.

GLORIA: Oh shit, now I've pissed her off. (running after her) Mattie, I'm sorry, I didn't mean it like that. (as Mattie ignores her; exits) Please, Mattie, I said I was sorry... C'mon now... don't be mad at me. You know I'm always saying dumb things I don't mean... (exits after Mattie)

    Jessica shakes her head in dismay, and wanders over to the drafting table in the corner by the sliding glass doors. Curious to know what Harry's writing, she starts nosing through the pages scattered atop the table.

    Harry enters through a side door leading to the sundeck. He sees Jessica reading his work and has a fit.

HARRY: Hey! What the hell you doing? Get away from there!

    Jessica turns and shrugs, unfazed by his irritation.

JESSICA: Okay, don't freak out. I was just looking at what you're writing.

    As Harry quickly covers up the pages.

What's the big deal? This is a daytime soap script, not top secret FBI documents y'know.

HARRY (irritated): It's my work and it's private, that's all you need to know.

JESSICA: Oooo, aren't we pissy today. What's the matter, genius, aren't you getting any?

> Harry ignores her and, with his foot, presses a button on the floor that automatically closes the drapes, hiding the view.

JESSICA: I guess that's my cue to leave you alone, huh? (when Harry, still miffed, doesn't answer) Look, if I've really offended you, I'm sorry. You're right. This *is* your house, and I am a guest here, and I shouldn't be nosing around your—

HARRY (softening): Aw, forget it. (pecks her on the cheek) I'm sorry. You're right, it's no big deal. Nothing I write nowadays is worth being off-limits, anyway—especially to you. It's just... oh, hell, I dunno... guess I'm just getting crotchety in my old age.

> Jessica smiles fondly, gives him a hug, and kisses his nose.

JESSICA: Not you, Harry. You're never gonna get old. When the rest of us are sitting around here in our nineties, looking like dried-up old prunes, you'll still look like you did that first day I saw you, coming in off the beach, that dumb fishing pole in your hand, and grinning like a boy 'cause you'd caught that teeny little fish.

HARRY: Little? My dear Jessica, that fish was big enough to swallow a whale. (grins as he reflects) It was kinda small, wasn't it?

JESSICA: I've seen bigger sardines.

HARRY: Well, it was my first fish.

JESSICA: And your last, if I remember the look you gave when Mattie insisted you clean it yourself.

HARRY (grimaces as he recalls): Man, talk about the sudden demise of a new hobby. (as it hits him) Is that how you really remember me?

JESSICA: Absolutely. I thought here is the cutest, most adorable guy I've ever seen... Course, the sun was in my eyes at the time, so—

HARRY: There was no sun. I caught that monster at the crack of dawn. (as it hits him) What were you doing here at that ungodly hour, anyway?

JESSICA: Obeying your instructions, remember? You told Gloria to get me here very early so we could drive to Santa Barbara for breakfast and the art festival.

HARRY: I did? But the art festival lasts all day.

JESSICA: My words, exactly. I know, Gloria said, but Harry's kind of a weird duck when it comes to crowds.

HARRY: Oh-h-h... yeah... now I remember.

JESSICA: And moi, being the eager-beaver, beauty queen from little ol' Prairie View, was so anxious to meet the big-time Hollywood writer Glo-Worm had described you as... well, I couldn't get here early enough.

HARRY: Man, that's right. I did tell Gloria that. Good memory, babe.

JESSICA (with fondness): Good memories, period. (beat of sadness for both) God, those were fun times, weren't they?

HARRY: The best. Don't think I ever laughed so much in all my life.

JESSICA: Me, either. (perplexed) Sure turned sour in a hurry, though, didn't it?

HARRY: Yeah. You know I was thinking about us the other day—wondering what happened. I mean, two people couldn't have been more in love.

JESSICA: True.

HARRY: So, what happened?

JESSICA: I grew up, remember?

HARRY: And I didn't.

JESSICA: Something like that. (reflects wistfully) When you've just turned twenty and you're from Podunk, Texas, the world seems like one giant playground. Which is kind of cruel really because it's anything but. (small laugh) And, after a few years and a lot of slaps in the face, you suddenly realize that all too clearly... and sometimes, just a little too late.

HARRY (thinking aloud): How sad. (rests his hands on her shoulders) I'm sorry if I hurt you. I never intended to—you must believe that.

JESSICA: I never thought you did. Well, maybe a little at first, right after you dumped me. But then, as I got older and had time to think about it, I realized what you wanted and what I wanted was completely opposite. I mean, the truth is, the marriage was doomed from the start, and we were lucky it didn't go on and on with us ending up hating each other.

HARRY: I guess.

JESSICA: Hey, don't sound so glum. We're still buddies, aren't we? That's more than most ex-husbands and ex-wives can say, right?

HARRY: I guess.

JESSICA: And if I hadn't have got divorced I probably wouldn't have needed therapy, and if I hadn't gone to therapy I wouldn't have realized how much I liked it and become who I am today.

HARRY (wry): So you owe me big-time, that what you're saying?

JESSICA: More than you'll ever know. On top of that, I like you better now than when we first met, and I thought you were sexiest hunk alive.

HARRY (straight-faced): I still am the sexiest hunk alive. (fondly taps her chin with his fist) And don't you ever forget it.

> They look at each other; then, as if on a silent signal, clinch.

JESSICA: Oh, Harry...

> He kisses her on the head as they remain clinched.

GLORIA (entering from kitchen with a café latte): Hey, hey, hey, what's going on here?

> Jessica and Harry guiltily break apart, even though there's no reason they should feel that way.

GLORIA (half-joking to Jessica): You stole my man once, you round-heels hussy, let's not be doing it again. Especially not right under my adorable little nose.

JESSICA: I didn't steal him, Glo', you <u>introduced</u> him to me, remember? Told me to take my best shot.

GLORIA: A decision I'll always regret. Little Miss Matchmaker Gloria, that's me. (to Harry) Next time you're lonely, buddy, and want someone to take to dinner, go ask one of your <u>other</u> ex-wives to fix you up, okay?

HARRY (grins): From your lips to my heart. (jerks his thumb at the door to the sundeck) Now, if you guys don't mind, I've got work to do.

>   He heads for his writing table, and without sitting (he writes standing up) he begins to sort through the loose pages atop it.

GLORIA (to Jessica): Looks like we've got our walking papers, J.D. Care to join me out on the sundeck?

JESSICA: Be right there—soon as I've changed.

>   She heads off upstairs, and Gloria goes to the sundeck. Harry watches them exit with a troubled frown.

>   Lights dim.

Scene 3

When the lights come up, we're on the big sundeck that adjoins the house on the left side. It's a glorious day and the hot sun beats down on Jessica and Gloria. Both wear sunglasses and look beautifully tanned in their bikinis—their bodies glistening with lotion as they sunbathe on two of several sun loungers. With big-brimmed floppy hats protecting their faces from the sun, the women talk above the soft Jazz being piped outdoors from the house.

JESSICA: Did you notice Mr. H seemed a bit crabby today?

GLORIA: No more than usual, no. Why, what'd he say to you?

JESSICA: It wasn't what he said, but the way he said it. Like he was really on edge about something.

GLORIA: Probably just stressed out.

JESSICA: Y'think?

GLORIA: He's a writer. What more do I have to say?

JESSICA: I guess. But how stressful can it be to write a daytime soap? I mean, you watch them—it isn't exactly brain surgery, is it?

GLORIA: Maybe that's the problem. You know our Harry. He loves a good challenge, and maybe soap writing isn't doing it for him.

JESSICA: But it's steady money. Something that even for the short time we were married, I realized was an ongoing problem—for Harry and almost every writer—'cept maybe the guys at the very top. (as it hits her) Was Harry ever at the very top? When you guys were together, I mean?

GLORIA: No. He was doing okay, but nothing spectacular. He saved his peak years 'til after we were divorced.

JESSICA: You make it sound like he did it deliberately.

GLORIA: There were times when I thought he did. You know, just to spite me. But, of course, he didn't. I was just pissed that I married him at the wrong time—financially, at least... But after a few bumpy years apart, when I'd passed the bar, and we'd become friends again, I realized it was just all his hard work finally paying off, and I forgave him. (sarcastic) Noble of me, huh?

JESSICA (mind elsewhere): Harry once told me that only a tiny percent of the whole Writer's Guild makes a living—the rest have to support themselves with other jobs.

GLORIA: That's why Harry considers himself a lucky guy. He's never sold scripts for millions of dollars, but he's supported himself as a writer for better than twenty years (referring to the surroundings)—and not too badly, either.

> She pauses and peeks from under her hat as the sundeck door opens and out steps Abby, wearing sunglasses and a man's shirt over a red-and-white polka dot bikini. She carries a beach bag.

Well, lookee here, if it ain't Dr. Quincy herself.

ABBY: Careful, Glo', you're dating yourself. CSI's all the rage today.

GLORIA: Haven't you heard of reruns, child?

ABBY: Don't have time for late-night TV. I'm too busy carving up cadavers.

JESSICA (from under her hat): Hi, Abby.

ABBY: Hi, J.D.

GLORIA: I was wondering if you were gonna show up.

ABBY: It's Saturday, isn't it?

GLORIA: Yeah, but with the long weekend and all, I figured you'd be spending it with Brett.

ABBY (irked): That was the original plan. But then, as usual, an emergency came up, and he had to fly to San Francisco for the weekend.

JESSICA: Why didn't you go with him?

ABBY: And watch him work?

JESSICA: He can't work all the time, surely?

ABBY: You don't know Brett.

GLORIA: No, you've deliberately denied us all that pleasure by keeping him hidden from us. (needling) Why is that, doctor? Are you afraid one of us is going to hit on him?

> Abby ignores her. Sitting on the lounger, she positions her body to the best angle of the sun and rubs on suntan oil.

JESSICA: Seriously, Abby, when are we gonna meet him?

ABBY: As soon as I can drag him away from his magic markers and drawing board—which may actually be never.

GLORIA: Uh-oh, do I smell trouble in paradise?

ABBY: No, just coconut oil. (finishes oiling herself, then to Jessica) I bumped into Mattie on the way in and she said you were thinking of calling off the wedding. Is that true?

JESSICA (takes her hat off, angrily sits up): No, it's not true. Damn that woman!

ABBY: Don't have a cow. Knowing Mattie, I didn't believe her anyway.

JESSICA: Thank you for that.

GLORIA: So we should be expecting wedding invitations, exactly when?

JESSICA: When I get around to mailing them! (beat) And not a fucking second sooner. Okay?

GLORIA (exchanges raised-eyebrow looks with Abby): Oka-a-ay.

JESSICA (lies back, covers her face with the hat, muttering): God, I hate that woman.

ABBY: No, you don't. Mattie's like Harry. She's annoying as hell yet at the same time as lovable as your favorite teddy bear. I don't know how they do it, but they do. No matter how much they piss you off, sooner or later you forgive them. You can't help it. Staying mad at them is impossible.

JESSICA: You stayed mad at Harry long enough to get divorced.

ABBY: Thank you for reminding of that, J.D.

JESSICA: I'm sorry. I didn't mean it like it sounded.

GLORIA: What, catty as hell?

ABBY (ignoring Gloria): I know you didn't. It's the truth, anyway.

GLORIA: Uh-oh. Do I detect a tone of regret?

ABBY: Probably. But that's because I always thought I'd wait until I found exactly the right guy then marry him and stay married for the rest of my life. Now that dream's down the tubes, and for some reason I can't figure out, it grates the hell out of me.

JESSICA: Aww, don't feel too bad. I had the same dream.

GLORIA: Was that <u>before</u> or <u>after</u> you humped your way to Hollywood?

JESSICA: Up yours, Gloria.

ABBY: Oh shush you two. It's too early to be clawing each other's eyes out.

JESSICA: I agree. Finish what you were saying, Abby.

ABBY: I don't remember what I was saying.

GLORIA: You were telling us how much you regretted divorcing Harry.

ABBY: Ha ha, very funny. What I was trying to say was that when you get divorced you tend to over-analyze. At least I did. You go over and over in your mind what happened, and when and how it went wrong, and how much of it was your fault, when, if you just stood back and waited 'til your emotions settled down, you'd see the whole picture a lot more clearly. It took me a while to see it, but I finally came to the conclusion that the reason I was so confused was, I kept wondering what <u>I'd</u> done wrong when I should have been blaming Harry.

GLORIA: You mean it was all Harry's fault?

ABBY: Not the way you're inferring, no. But, yes, Harry is the reason we all divorced him. No one can deny that.

GLORIA: That makes me feel <u>much</u> better.

ABBY: Look, you can be sarcastic all you like, but the simple truth is that Harry just isn't someone who a woman—any woman—can stay married to. No matter how much you love him.

JESSICA: Wow, what makes you say that?

ABBY: It's just my opinion.

GLORIA: So explain yourself. We're all ears.

ABBY: Remember that old Errol Flynn line Harry's always quoting? "Women won't let me stay single and I won't let me stay married." Well, Harry's living proof of it. He won't let himself stay married. Result is, after a while either he dumps you or he deliberately causes enough problems—consciously or subconsciously—so that you dump him.

JESSICA: Wow. You really think that's it?

ABBY: Like I said, it's just my opinion.

JESSICA: Wow, I never thought of that.

GLORIA: I think you're right, Abby. I never thought of it that way either, but that's exactly the reason. And it doesn't just pertain to marriage.

JESSICA: What d'you mean?

GLORIA: Harry once told me that for him, it's all about the chase. Going after something he has to have—that's what excites him. I never paid much attention to him at the time, which I should have. Because expectations being far greater than the prize, once Harry got what he wanted—be it a car he couldn't afford, a writing assignment he wasn't up for, or a woman he had to have—he didn't want it any more. At least not as much as he did when he thought he couldn't get it, and he put all his energies into proving—to himself and everyone else—that he could.

JESSICA: Wow.

GLORIA: Jess, if you say that one more time, I'm gonna throw you off the frigging sundeck—

She pauses as the sundeck door opens and Harry joins them. He looks like he belongs in Rome or Monte Carlo: aviator sunglasses, linen slacks, sport shirt, and a killer linen jacket.

The women look at him in disbelief.

GLORIA (to Jessica): What the hell are you waiting for? Now's the perfect time for one of your stupid wows.

JESSICA (ignores her; to Harry): You've got pants on.

HARRY: Course I've got pants on! This may be Malibu, but last time I heard, they throw you in jail you for going without them.

ABBY: She means you always wear shorts, smart ass.

JESSICA: Where're you going dressed like that?

HARRY (fake innocence): Like, what?

GLORIA: An Italian gigolo peacocking along the *Via Veneto*.

ABBY (aside): Ouch.

HARRY: Are you suggesting I normally look like a bum?

GLORIA: If you mean "beach bum," then yeah.

HARRY: I resent that. I may not always be an ad for Armani, but—

ABBY: For Christ's sake Harry, just answer the question.

HARRY: I'm picking someone up at the airport.

GLORIA: Well, Scarlet Johansson smokes and Kim Basinger's gotten too old for you, so it can't be either of them.

JESSICA: I've got it: Jessica Simpson's just flown in to beg you to write her life story.

HARRY: Hmm.

ABBY: Well? You gonna tell us who it is, or what?

HARRY (knows what he's going to say will cause an unfavorable reaction, but says it anyway): A friend.

   The word "friend" makes the women's scalp prickle.

JESSICA: "Friend"?

GLORIA: Friend, who? (as he hesitates) Come on, Harry, don't mess around. Who're you going to pick up?

HARRY: A girl—a woman I met on location in San Francisco.

   Instantly, all three ex-wives sit bolt upright, sun hats falling off, and they squint incredulously at Harry.

ABBY: A woman as in another writer woman or... (she stops, his smug look telling her everything) Oh-my-Gawd, you got a new girlfriend!

HARRY: You make it sound like I'm not entitled or that I need your permission.

GLORIA: What you need, is your goddamn head examined. You need another girlfriend like I need another wrinkle.

HARRY (to Jessica): You want to add anything?

GLORIA: He means other than wow.

JESSICA: How old is she?

HARRY (lying): I've no idea. You know how touchy your species is about revealing age.

GLORIA: Save the bullshit, Harry. How old is she?

> He shrugs and stays silent.

ABBY: Under or over eighteen?

HARRY: Eight-<u>teen</u>? What kind of guy you think I am?

ABBY: We know exactly what kind of guy you are. That's why we're asking. And if you really don't know, take a wild guess.

HARRY: Twenty, maybe. (as they all look at each other and roll their eyes) Oh shit, I gotta go. You know how traffic is going to LAX.

> He hurries into the house before they can pepper him with more questions. The women exchange "oh-my-God" looks once again, but can't find the words to describe how they feel. Then, finally:

JESSICA: What shall we do?

GLORIA: The only thing we can do. (as the women look at her) We'll have to do the poor girl a favor and shoot the bastard.

> Lights dim.

Scene 4

> Later. Beach house. Living room. The ex-wives, with shirts over their bikinis, have Mattie trapped against the drapes.

MATTIE: I'm telling you the truth. I didn't know Harry had a new girlfriend. He just told me 'bout her as he was leaving the house.

GLORIA: What exactly did he say? Think, Mattie. This could affect you as well, you know.

MATTIE (suspicious): How exactly?

GLORIA: Are you kidding me? Harry brings home some bimbo who thinks she's hooking up with a big Hollywood writer. She takes one look at you and decides you have to go so she can have the house all to herself in order to get her hooks into him.

MATTIE: It doesn't matter what <u>she</u> wants, Harry can't fire me. I come with the house remember? Got my own apartment downstairs.

ABBY: Calm down, Mattie. (as Gloria opens her mouth to speak) Shut-up, Glo. (to Mattie) All we're asking is: Did Harry mention who this woman is, or how they met, or how long she's planning to stay?

MATTIE: No, none of that. He just said he was gonna pick this friend of his up at LAX. And when I asked him what friend, he said nobody I knew, just some aerobics instructor he'd met on the set while he was up in 'Frisco.

> At the words "aerobics instructor," the three ex-wives react as if their worst fears have been confirmed.

JESSICA (barely audible): Aerobics instructor?

GLORIA: I hate her already.

MATTIE (answering Jessica): That's what he said. You know how Harry likes to work out, no matter where he goes.

ABBY: Yes, Mattie, we're all well aware of that fact. (as it suddenly hits her) My God, that's why he stopped by to see me.

JESSICA: What? When?

ABBY: My lab. Yesterday. Pretended he wanted to buy me dinner. I <u>knew</u> there was more to it than that. He just wanted to make sure I was coming today so he could spring his new girlfriend on me.

JESSICA: Why would he do that? Most guys would want their exes as far away from the house as possible.

GLORIA: My dear J.D., Harry is not most guys. In fact, he's not like any other guy, period. If he were, none of us would have married him or remained friends after divorcing him. (to Abby) He called me too. Said he knew this writer who needed an attorney and was I interested in representing him. When I tried to pin him down about what the guy had done, he said he'd know more by today and would tell me then. Bastard.

JESSICA (hurt): He never called me.

ABBY: Jess exactly how many summer weekends have you ever missed since Harry moved in here?

JESSICA: Not too many… and none since you and Harry broke up. (catching on) Oh-h. I see. Hey, that's kind of sneaky of him, isn't it?

MATTIE: I don't know why you're all getting so uptight. Harry's got a right to have a girlfriend, him being single and all.

    The three women ignore Mattie and exchange ominous looks. Then Gloria asks Mattie:

GLORIA: How much is it going to cost for you to fix the three of us one of your jumbo-deluxe shrimp salads with low-cal Thousand Island dressing?

MATTIE: Gloria, you know I don't take bribes.

GLORIA: Fifty bucks?

MATTIE (hooked, but playing it cool): If you're <u>that</u> hungry, I guess it would be kinda selfish of me to say no.

    She enters the kitchen. Abby and Jessica look at Gloria.

ABBY: What was <u>that</u> all about?

GLORIA: A, I wanted to keep her busy so she wouldn't hear what we're discussing, and B, I've a horrible feeling we're going to need all the energy we can get just to survive the barbecue this afternoon.

    Lights dim.

Scene 5

When the lights come up, we're in the living room of the beach house. The drapes are now open, and the ex-wives and Mattie all stand with their noses pressed against the windows flanking the front door, eagerly awaiting Harry to return with his new girlfriend. Outside, a car pulls up.

ABBY: Hide! Hide!

Mattie runs into the kitchen, the other women flee out the side door onto the sundeck. There are voices outside the front door.

Then the door opens, and in walks Harry and KIMBERLY WOODS. "Woodsy" as Harry calls her, is twenty and gorgeous, has a killer body and, big surprise—she's a brunette! She's also energetic and teeth-gratingly peppy—as only an aerobics instructor can be. She hangs on every word Harry says, which makes him—more than twenty-five years her senior—feel damn good about himself.

Kimberly looks around her, then out at the view in incredulous delight.

KIMBERLY: Oh-my-God, this is awesome!

She runs exuberantly across the room and does an acrobatic double-flip, landing on her feet by the sliding glass doors. Then without missing a beat (or seeing Harry's mouth drop open), she stands there gazing out at the beach.

Harry, recovering from the double flip, closes his mouth and the front door, and he joins Kimberly. She beams like a toothpaste ad.

I'd never leave here! I mean it, Harry. You couldn't pry me out of this house with a screwdriver! I'd set up my *Lifecycle* and treadmill right here (indicates window), my free weights here (indicates a few feet away), and do my yoga right here (indicates the corner by the window opposite Harry's writing table). God, I'd be set for life. The only time I'd go outside would be if I wanted to go swimming or jogging on the beach. (squeezes his arm) Or for one of those romantic walks in the moonlight you talked about.

HARRY (has his doubts about the outcome of her being around when he writes, but trying to be cool): That's great. I'm glad you like it.

KIMBERLY: Like it? I <u>love</u> it, Harry! It's totally cool!

   She flings her arms around him so enthusiastically it staggers him and he has to regain his balance.

Oh, God, we're gonna be sooooo happy here! Mmm-mmmm!

   She gives him a big kiss, steps back, and looks at the view again, just as Mattie comes out of the kitchen. Mattie takes one look at Kimberly and stops dead in her tracks, jaw dropping in surprise.

   Kimberly doesn't see her but Harry does, and he knows why Mattie is shocked. He pretends not to notice, however, and he begins the introductions.

HARRY: Hi, Mattie. I'd like you to meet Kimberly Woods. Kimberly, say hello to the Sheriff of Malibu: Mattie Fyne.

   Kimberly bounces over to Mattie and extends her hand like she's meeting an old friend.

KIMBERLY: Hi, Mattie. Great to meet you!

MATTIE (staring at Kimberly's black hair, she shakes her hand): You too. (still staring at her hair) Is that a wig?

The door to the sundeck opens a crack, and Abby, Jessica, and Gloria peer in. Their reaction to Kimberly's black hair—like Mattie's—is one of absolute shock.

KIMBERLY: N-No. (tugs on it) What makes you ask that?

HARRY (before Mattie can reply): Woodsy—I mean Kimberly—is gonna be staying here for a few weeks—

MATTIE (challengingly): Is that right?

KIMBERLY: Only if it's okay with you, Mattie? I mean, Harry said there was a spare bedroom nobody uses, and I promise (Girl Scouts' sign) I'll keep it clean and tidy.

MATTIE (knows she's being stroked but appreciates Kimberly's effort): You're more than welcome to use it. (gives Harry a withering glare) Be nice to have someone 'round here with manners for a change.

She goes back in the kitchen. Harry winks at Kimberly.

HARRY: Like I said, she hates me with a passion.

KIMBERLY: Why do you keep her on, then?

HARRY: She came with the place. Lives downstairs in what used to be the laundry room. The original owners turned it into a little apartment. (shrugs) Anyway, having Mattie around keeps me on my toes. And so long as she treats you okay, I'm cool with it.

KIMBERLY (dotingly): Then I don't care either. (cuddles up to him) Just so long as she doesn't make late-night bed checks or anything. I mean, I'd hate her to find mine empty and ruin your reputation.

HARRY (kisses her nose): What reputation?

> They kiss, before Harry leads her towards the stairs. There, Kimberly faces Harry, puts her arms around his neck and rubs her nose against his.

KIMBERLY: Did I tell you that you've made me the happiest girl alive?

HARRY (deadpans): Not more than a hundred times.

KIMBERLY: Well, get used to it, lover, 'cause I'm just getting warmed up.

> She kisses him passionately. He responds. The kiss goes on and on until we wonder if they're ever coming up for air. Finally they separate, and Harry—not as young as he used to be—looks exhausted.

HARRY (still gulping in air, he leads her upstairs): Kimberly, before you kill an old man, I think I'd better show you your room.

> Once Harry and Kimberly are out of sight, the sundeck door opens and the three ex-wives sneak in. They creep to the stairs and look up, to make sure Harry and Kimberly are gone.

KIMBERLY'S VOICE (from upstairs bedroom, sexy): Take it slow'n easy. I want you to last a hundred years.

> The ex-wives roll their eyes and swap looks of consternation.

GLORIA: Kimberly? Dimberly more like it. A brunette? Our boy's in a lot of trouble, you know that, don't you?

JESSICA: You know it, and we know it, but does Harry know it?

ABBY: Not if that kiss is any indication. Jesus, that girl must've gone to diving school.

GLORIA: And never used an oxygen tank!

JESSICA: God, I expected poor ole Harry to collapse at any moment.

GLORIA: Or gag on her tongue.

ABBY: Not him. His vanity wouldn't let him do either.

GLORIA: That's why he's in trouble. Poor dumb bastard. The way she's got him twisted round her little finger, he can't see the forest for the trees.

JESSICA: What does that mean, anyway? I've always wondered.

GLORIA: Well, it ain't good news, that's for sure. (goes to the wet bar and grabs a bottle) I don't know about you guys, but I need a serious drink.

JESSICA: Little early for vodka, isn't it?

GLORIA: My emotions don't know what time it is. (to Abby) Join me?

ABBY: After what we've just seen, gladly.

JESSICA: I suppose this does qualify as an emergency.

GLORIA: More like a fucking disaster. (holds up bottle to Jessica) You with us, Goldilocks?

JESSICA: Oh-why-not.

    Gloria fixes three drinks and passes them around. Toasts:

GLORIA: To us blondes—Harry's only hope for survival.

ABBY (chuckles): That may be a little extreme, but...

They clink glasses and drink, Gloria the heartiest.

JESSICA (reflects): Do you think he <u>really</u> likes her?

GLORIA: Sweetie, this is so way past "like" it isn't funny. Harry's so hot for Miss Hard Buns, he's probably ready to pop the question.

ABBY: If he hasn't already.

JESSICA: Get out.

GLORIA: How else do you explain this sudden phenomenon?

JESSICA: I can't. But one thing I do know: Harry's never gonna get married again. He told me so himself, a zillion times.

GLORIA: Told me the same thing. But that was before today and what we just witnessed. (to Abby) You know him best, what's your take on it?

ABBY: Mind-boggling. As long as I've known Harry, he's never even looked at a brunette—gorgeous or otherwise—let alone brought one home.

JESSICA: I agree. I once said I was thinking of dyeing my hair. Nothing drastic—you know, just a strawberry blonde shade—and I thought he was gonna have a conniption.

ABBY: Knowing Harry, I'm surprised he didn't.

GLORIA (gloomily): Death, taxes, and Harry's blondes: they were the three things I could always rely on. And now—pooof!—one of 'em's dust!

She drains her drink, pours another, and gulps most of it.

JESSICA: Hey, take it easy. We have a whole day ahead of us.

ABBY: You think maybe. . .? Nah. Couldn't be.

JESSICA: Couldn't be what?

GLORIA (when Abby doesn't reply): Abby, this is no time to get secretive. If you know something we don't, spit it out.

ABBY: I was just thinking—wondering—if Harry could be playing a joke on us. You know what a warped sense of humor he has.

GLORIA: I'd love to believe that, but I'm afraid it's just wishful thinking.

ABBY: Probably. But it's the only rational explanation I can think of.

JESSICA: Now it all makes sense. You know, why he wanted all of us to be here when he brought her home. He wanted us to see his new wife.

ABBY: No, it must be just a big joke. I refuse to believe it's true.

GLORIA: Well a joke would account for why he's never mentioned her before.

ABBY (thinking aloud): Wonder if he's told Lila?

GLORIA (immediately bristling): Lila? What would she have to do with it?

ABBY: Nothing. But we all know Harry confides in her at times.

JESSICA: Let's call her and find out.

GLORIA: You call her if you want, but I'm having nothing to do with that shitty bitch.

ABBY: Whoa! Since when did Lila become a shitty bitch?

GLORIA: Since the first time I met her.

JESSICA: I didn't know you hated Lila.

GLORIA: Well, now you do. So shut up about her, okay?

   She fixes herself another drink, and gulps some of it down.

JESSICA: I've only met her a few times, but I thought she was pretty nice. I liked her, in fact.

GLORIA: You like everybody.

JESSICA: No I don't. (to Abby) You like her too, don't you?

ABBY: From the little I know her, sure. She can be snooty sometimes, but fortunately, by the time Harry and I hooked up, Lila had already remarried and was out of the picture.

GLORIA: Lucky you. When I married Harry, she was still single and hoping to get him back. Jesus, every time I turned around she was all over the guy like ugly on an elk.

JESSICA: Ape.

GLORIA: What?

JESSICA: It's "ugly on an ape," not elk. Elk are beautiful creatures.

GLORIA: Good. Go fuck one. Probably the only thing you haven't slept with by now, anyway.

   She grabs the vodka and storms out onto the sundeck.

JESSICA: Man, what's her problem?

ABBY: Ever heard of the menopause?

JESSICA: At thirty-eight?

ABBY: Hits some earlier than others.

MATTIE'S VOICE (from the kitchen): Menopause ain't her problem.

ABBY (to kitchen door): Mattie, if you want in on this conversation, at least have the decency to come out and join us.

    Mattie emerges from the kitchen with the air of one grievously misjudged.

MATTIE: I wasn't eavesdropping, so don't think I was. You guys were talking so loud a person would have to be deaf not to hear every word.

JESSICA: So if it isn't the menopause what is it?

MATTIE: She just flat-out hates Lila.

JESSICA: Why?

MATTIE: Blames her for busting her and Harry up.

JESSICA: Really? I didn't know that.

MATTIE: Honey, what you don't know 'bout Harry and Gloria would stretch all the way to New York 'n' back.

JESSICA (to Abby): Did you know?

ABBY: Not all the details, but, yeah, I did know Glo' blamed Lila for Harry dumping her. (to Mattie) Had something to do with Gloria helping Lila move, right?

MATTIE: Helping her move and, at the same time, never telling Lila that her and Harry were already heating up the same sheets.

JESSICA: So what happened?

MATTIE: When Harry and Lila split up, she needed to move her stuff into a new apartment and asked him to help her out. He couldn't help 'cause he had a meeting with a producer that day, but said he'd find someone to take his place.

JESSICA: And he sent Gloria over? Wow, that's pretty ballsy.

MATTIE: Stupid's more like it. But that's Harry for you: never thinks past his you-know-what, 'cept when it comes to his writing.

JESSICA: Amen.

ABBY: Knowing Harry, he probably thought he was doing Lila a favor.

JESSICA: By having his new girlfriend help his old wife to move? Come on! Even Harry isn't that naïve.

ABBY: Don't bet on it.

MATTIE: He might've gotten away with it too, if Lila hadn't needed a friendly shoulder to cry on. The poor girl spilled her heart out: told Gloria all about how she still loved Harry and wanted to get him back. Of course Gloria just let her ramble on and on, never once stopping her. Never once saying that she and Harry were already a hot item and there was no chance in hell Lila was gonna get him back—

JESSICA: Oooooh, big mistake.

ABBY: And then some.

MATTIE: 'Course, Gloria kept her mouth shut and her ears open, same as she always does when it's to her benefit. And then, later, she couldn't wait to run back to Harry and tell him everything.

JESSICA: Wow, what'd he say?

MATTIE: Nothing. Harry's a lot of things, but mean and spiteful ain't one of 'em. (sighs)

JESSICA: So what happened next?

MATTIE: The next day was Saturday, which just happened to be Harry's birthday. Lila, bless her heart, thought she'd surprise him and deliver his present personally, hoping that he'd changed his mind, that she could persuade him to get the marriage back on track.

ABBY: Yep, and she marched right into this very house and found him humpin' Glo-Worm.

JESSICA: Oh to be a fly on <u>that</u> wall.

ABBY: You would've been squashed by flying furniture—if what I heard is true.

MATTIE: It was some big go-around all right. The Thriller in Manila Part Two, Harry calls it.

JESSICA: Wonder who won?

ABBY: Nobody. In a situation like that, everyone loses. From that point on, Lila vowed to make Gloria's life a misery.

JESSICA: Even when they got married?

MATTIE: Especially when they got married. Lila did everything she could to split them up, until finally she succeeded, and Gloria's blamed her ever since.

    Harry comes downstairs, asking:

HARRY: Blamed who for what?

    He joins the women, who look at him like he's a stranger.

HARRY: What, what, what?

ABBY: Girl talk, Harry. Just girl talk.

HARRY: Oh. (to Mattie) So what d'you think of Kimberly? Is she a knockout or what?

MATTIE: I wouldn't know, Harry. I was too busy trying to get over her hair to see what she looked like.

ABBY (gives Jessica a play-along-with-me look): Hair? Whose hair?

HARRY: Kimberly's—my new girlfriend.

ABBY (fake innocence): Oh she's here already?

HARRY: Upstairs, showering and changing clothes. I'll introduce you, soon as she comes down.

JESSICA: What's wrong with her hair?

MATTIE: It's black.

   Abby and Jessica fake their shock, then together:

ABBY/JESSICA: You're-dating-a-brunette?

HARRY: What's wrong with that?

ABBY: Nothing's <u>wrong</u> with it, Harry. But considering your track record, you must admit it's unusual to say the least.

GLORIA: How about fucking bizarre?

   She enters from the sundeck, half-empty bottle of vodka in hand, no glass, and she's a little drunk.

JESSICA: Bizarre's good.

HARRY: What's bizarre about a girl having black hair? Millions of girls have black hair.

As he's speaking, Gloria hugs Jessica and kisses her cheek.

GLORIA: Sorry 'bout what I said earlier. I was just being an asshole, as usual. Forgive me?

JESSICA: 'Course, silly.

Gloria confronts Harry, tone belligerent, as:

GLORIA: Okay, so let's cut the shit and get to the chase. Why the big switch over? What's the matter; no blondes left to fuck in California?

HARRY: You're drunk, Glo'.

GLORIA: And I intend to get drunker. So, unless you want me to bounce this bottle off your head, you'd better come up with an answer.

Harry steps back, not trusting her unpredictable temper.

HARRY: I... uh... just decided it was time to make a change. I keep bombing out with blondes, so I thought I'd give the other end of the spectrum a shot. (to Abby and Jessica) Wait 'til you meet her. Then you'll know exactly why I love her.

ABBY: I'm afraid I'll have to take your word for it. (to the others) See you guys later.

She starts away towards the sundeck, but Harry stops her.

HARRY: Whoa, where you going?

ABBY: To get my things. Then I'm going home.

HARRY: Home? But why? You haven't been here that long.

ABBY: Long enough.

HARRY: But you'll miss the barbecue.

ABBY: I'll take a rain check. (heading towards the door) Bye all.

HARRY: No, wait! (grabs her arm) I want you to meet Kimberly.

ABBY: Why?

HARRY: Because… I… I value your opinion. (includes others) All of you. I want to see if you think she's the right girl for me.

   The three ex-wives are silent a beat, then:

ABBY: Sorry, Harry. This is one decision you'll have to make on your own. (pecks him on the cheek) You're a big boy now. You're perfectly capable of knowing what you want.

   She exits to the sundeck. Harry turns to the others, desperate and not really understanding what has just happened.

HARRY: Don't let her go. (when they don't respond) Please, it's important.

JESSICA: To you, maybe. But apparently not to Abby.

   She exits after Abby.

GLORIA: Poor-old-Harry. Losing your touch, are you?

   She exits after Jessica. Harry grips Mattie's arm.

HARRY: You gotta help me. Abby'll listen to you.

MATTIE: Harry, like you tell me all the time, it's not up to me who comes and who goes in this house.

HARRY: Mattie, please.

MATTIE: But even if it *was* up to me, and I *was* trying to help you, I not only wouldn't stop those fine ladies from leaving but I'd kick their butts out the door and tell them they couldn't come back again. Ever.

HARRY: I thought you liked them.

MATTIE: Oh, I like 'em all right—especially Abby.

HARRY: Then what?

MATTIE: It ain't healthy, Harry. Not for you, not for them.

HARRY: Oh Mattie, not that again.

MATTIE: When a man divorces a woman, it means he doesn't want her in his life no more. At least, that's what it *should* mean—and does mean for most people. And if you're as smart as you say, you'll understand that and get on with your life. (indicates upstairs) Especially if you plan on setting up shop with that young 'un. And you do, don't you?

HARRY (not too convincingly): Sure, but—

MATTIE: Then do like I say. Show those pretty women the door and tell 'em they're not welcome here again. Then maybe—if you're serious—you and Kimberly can start working on your future.

    She returns to the kitchen. Harry heaves a sigh.

HARRY (thinking aloud): I could never do that.

KIMBERLY'S VOICE (from upstairs): Oh Harry. Snookums, can you come up here a sec?

HARRY: Coming.

He goes upstairs. The kitchen door opens, and Mattie pokes her head out, looks after Harry and mutters in disbelief:

MATTIE: "Snookums?"

Lights dim.

Scene 6

Lights come up. We're on the sundeck. Abby is stuffing her towel and suntan lotion into her beach bag, while Jessica and Gloria try to reason with her.

JESSICA: Abby, you can't leave now. You haven't even met the woman.

ABBY: I don't want to meet her. I just wanna get the hell out of here.

GLORIA: If you won't stay for Harry then stay for us. We need you.

JESSICA: Glo's right. You can't walk out on something as important as this and leave us to deal with it.

ABBY: Watch me.

GLORIA: What happened to that Three Musketeers "all-for-one-one-for-all" crap you're always preaching?

ABBY: I left it at home—along with my wedding ring and drawer full of heartaches.

JESSICA: But you're the only one of us Harry listens to. You run out now and you know what's gonna happen? He's gonna end up marrying that… that… gym rat.

GLORIA: Jessica's right. Do you want that on your conscience?

ABBY (exasperated): First of all, I think you're getting way ahead of yourselves. Just because Harry brought home a hottie who doesn't fit the usual profile doesn't mean he plans on marrying her.

GLORIA: Well that's not what you were saying earlier. And what about (mimicking Kimberly's voice) "Take it slow 'n easy. I want you to last for a hundred years."

ABBY: That's her perspective, not Harry's.

JESSICA: Are you forgetting that hour-long kiss?

ABBY: A lot of dots have to be connected between kissing and saying I do. (shrugs) Anyway, like I told him earlier: he's a big boy and perfectly capable of making his own decisions. So, what happens next certainly won't be on my conscience.

> She turns away. Jessica starts to grab at her, but Gloria stops her.

GLORIA: Forget it, J.D. Let her go. If she wants to abandon Harry when he needs her most, that's her prerogative. (to Abby) But remember this: I know why you're really going. You're still in love with Harry and can't stand to see him fawning over another woman.

ABBY (angry because it's true): Bullshit! I stopped loving Harry two years ago: when he forced me to get a divorce.

GLORIA: Then prove it. Stick around and help the poor dumb bastard realize he's making an idiot of himself before it's too late.

ABBY: Why should I?

GLORIA: 'Cause the guy's having a fucking mid-life crisis, that's why! And because, despite being a royal pain in the ass most of the time, he's been there for us—all of us—whenever we've needed him.

> There's truth in that, and Abby hesitates, mulling it over.

JESSICA: Glo's right, you know.

ABBY: Oh, so now you're an expert on having a mid-life crisis?

JESSICA: I'm not an expert on anything.

GLORIA: That's not what I heard.

JESSICA: That's not even funny. (to Abby) I'm not saying I know much about crises of any kind, but I do know that, according to Harry, since high school he's been chasing, screwing, and marrying only blondes. Blondes who, a shrink once told him—

ABBY: I know, I know, "who remind Harry of his math teacher, one Katherine Holroyde, who he had the crush-to-end-all-crushes on and who—for reasons he never knew—hated his guts. So?

JESSICA: So, the shrink said that it all added up to Harry's feelings being left in a perpetual pause mode. An unfinished cycle is the correct psychological term, and he's been trying to complete it ever since."

ABBY: This is all very informative, but what are you getting at?

JESSICA: So now, on the eve of his forty-eighth birthday, he does a three-sixty overnight and brings home a brunette: a creature normally so far off Harry's Richter scale he wouldn't have noticed her if she'd walked past him bare-ass naked. A brunette, I repeat, who's young enough to be his goddamn granddaughter.

ABBY: Big deal. Harry's always gone for young chicks—or have you forgotten how young we all were when we married him?

JESSICA: Young's one thing, cradle-snatching's another.

GLORIA: Which brings up another vital point: Even if you're not worried about Harry's downfall, think about hers. She's still a baby. Probably has the same dream you had: marrying Mr. Right and living happily ever after. If we don't put the kibosh on this fiasco, that poor girl can kiss her dream goodbye and will most likely hate herself for the rest of her life.

ABBY: My God, Glo', wait a minute and I'll cue up the violins.

GLORIA: Sorry, vodka always makes me melodramatic. But it's not that far-fetched, even you gotta admit.

ABBY: I admit nothing. I still think both of you are jumping the gun. Think about it. Harry was only in San Francisco at the end of last month. That means, even if they met the day he arrived—which I doubt—they've only known each other two weeks. Probably less. Even Harry wouldn't jump into marriage after only fourteen days.

GLORIA: Oh no? He married Lila after only knowing her four months; me, a week less than that—

JESSICA: And *moi*, after only three months—

ABBY (as they look at her accusingly): Okay, so I married him after ten weeks, which was obviously a mistake I wouldn't make again. But ten weeks is a far cry from only two.

GLORIA: You're missing the point. Can't you see, each time he's gotten married he's known the girl for less time. Two weeks, three weeks, even four weeks; what difference does it make? This is Harry we're talking about. The man whose heroes are Errol Flynn and Clark Gable for God's sake! A guy who believes in love at first sight; who's on a first-name basis with half the wedding chapels in Las Vegas; and who follows up "hi, my name's Harry Spain," with "I do," and a trip down the fucking aisle.

JESSICA: He's also the only guy I know who loves the NFL and NASCAR but cries while watching *An Affair to Remember*—

ABBY: Okay, okay, enough already.

GLORIA: Then you'll stay and help us?

ABBY: Whoa, I didn't say that. First I wanna know something: What if you're wrong? What if Harry does just want to get laid? What happens then?

GLORIA: <u>Then</u> I'll owe you an apology and we'll all go home thankful. But knowing Harry as I do, I like my chances.

JESSICA: All we're asking you to do is stay long enough to see if we're right. And if we are, to help us bring Harry to his senses before he jumps headfirst into another failed marriage—something that at his age he can't afford, emotionally, or financially.

    Abby sighs, ready to give in but still not sure they're right.

ABBY: Oka-ay. But on one condition.

GLORIA: Name it.

ABBY: If, at any time before Harry gets around to burning the hamburger buns, we see any indication that his head isn't up his ass and he has no intention of leading Ms. Hard Buns to the altar, I'm out of here, and you guys are on the hook for the most expensive lunch I can find. Deal?

GLORIA AND JESSICA (together): Deal.

    They all raise their hands and slap high-fives.

GLORIA: Now, let's put our heads together and come up with a plan to derail this train before it gets a chance to leave the station.

    Lights dim. Curtain.

END OF ACT ONE

WIFE FIVE

ACT TWO
Scene 1

> Curtain rises. Lights come up. We're on the sundeck. Harry and his exes are enjoying burgers, corn, potato salad, and beer, while Kimberly picks at a salad.

KIMBERLY: Lover, this salad dressing's awesome!

HARRY: Thanks. But Mattie deserves all the credit: it's her secret recipe. (to the others) How're your burgers?

GLORIA (mimicking Kimberly): Awesome, lover. Just awesome.

> Awkward silence, broken by Abby, who turns to Kimberly:

ABBY: Harry says you and he met on the set of his last picture.

KIMBERLY: Yes. I was there to give the director a massage and—

GLORIA: Whoa, massage? I thought you were an aerobics instructor?

KIMBERLY: I am. I'm also a state-certified masseuse and fitness trainer. I'm getting a lot of clients too—my Uncle Nick has been very good to me, putting me in touch with people in the industry.

JESSICA: Uncle Nick?

HARRY: Oh didn't I tell you, Kimberly's uncle is Nicolas Cage.

JESSICA: The actor?

KIMBERLY (ecstatic): The one and only.

GLORIA (to Abby): So now it all starts to make sense. (she turns her attention to Harry) Sweetheart, why didn't you tell us your latest squeeze was so highly connected?

HARRY (immune to her sarcasm): I didn't think you'd be interested.

KIMBERLY: "Squeeze"—that's a gangster term isn't it, from the old days?

HARRY (grins) Glo-Worm's older than she looks.

GLORIA: Fuck you, Harry—

> A cell phone BUZZES. In comical unison Abby, Jessica, Gloria, and Kimberly reach for their purses.

HARRY: Relax guys, it's mine. (digs out his cell, checks the read-out, and rises) Excuse me. I gotta take this.

> Going to the railing, he answers the call.

JESSICA (to Abby and Gloria): When did Harry get a cell phone?

ABBY: Beats me. He always swore he'd never use one.

KIMBERLY: I bought it for him. (off their surprise) Why? What's the big deal?

GLORIA: Buying it is one thing, getting him to use it is another.

JESSICA: Just how did you persuade him, if you don't mind my asking?

KIMBERLY: I told him if he didn't use it, everyone would think he was one of those stubborn old farts who hated change.

ABBY: That must've amused him.

KIMBERLY: He was okay with it. In fact, once I taught him how to use it, he started calling people right away.

GLORIA: I underestimated you. (shrewdly) What else did you teach him?

Just then Harry returns.

HARRY: That was my agent. Says Max Fischer's over budget on his latest film and wants me to rewrite some scenes by tomorrow. Sorry ladies, but I have to go inside and leave you to soak up the sun by yourselves.

KIMBERLY: (disappointed): But I thought we were going to hang out together today. (she puts her arms around his neck and whispers in his ear) And you promised me a bit more "Harry loving" this afternoon.

GLORIA (loudly): Harry loving?

She pretends to stick her fingers down her throat, while Kimberly removes her arms from Harry's neck, visibly embarrassed by Gloria's reaction.

HARRY: Now, now Gloria, just because you're not getting any "Harry loving," there's no need to take it out on Kimberly. (turning to Kimberly) Don't worry, we'll spend time together later I promise.

KIMBERLY: But I'll miss you.

GLORIA: Oh for God's sake, he's just going inside, not off to war.

HARRY (laughing): Don't worry Woodsy, I won't be that long. Stay with the girls, finish your salad, and top up your tan. It'll be fun.

He kisses her on the forehead and goes indoors. There's an awkward silence as the women sit there alone.

GLORIA (gulps down her drink): How very fun for us.

Lights dim.

Scene 2

> Lights come up. Moments later. We're in the living room. Harry is sorting through some papers on the table, while Kimberly has come in from the sundeck and is pacing up and down.

HARRY (weakly): Gloria doesn't hate you—

KIMBERLY: Then why's she being so bitchy? I haven't done anything to her.

HARRY: Don't worry about it, she's just a grouch.

KIMBERLY: Y-You're not... not.... still sleeping with her, are you?

HARRY (surprised): Gloria? Christ, no! Don't be ridiculous. And I'm not sleeping with Abby or Jessica either, in case you're wondering. We're just friends.

KIMBERLY: Men and women can't be friends, everyone knows that.

HARRY: What is this, "When Harry Met Sally?"

KIMBERLY: Sally? Who is she? Not another ex-wife?

HARRY (amused): No! "When Harry Met Sally." It's a movie. (Kimberly shakes her head) Y'know, Meg Ryan? Billy Crystal? Fake orgasms?

KIMBERLY: Never heard of it. Is it recent?

HARRY: Kind of. 1989. Something like that.

KIMBERLY (laughing): Harry honey that was before I was even born! Maybe my mom's heard of it. I could ring her... (she flips open her cell phone)

>Harry shakes his head in exasperation. He takes the phone from her and puts his arms around Kimberly's neck.

HARRY: Look, don't worry about "When Harry Met Sally," it's not important. The point is: I'm not sleeping with anyone but you. You do believe me don't you?

KIMBERLY: I'm sorry, Harry... Of course I believe you. It's just—

HARRY: What?

KIMBERLY: Oh, I dunno. Nothing. Everything. Your ex-wives, this house—

HARRY: I thought you loved the house?

KIMBERLY: I do, I do. It's totally awesome...

HARRY: But?

KIMBERLY: I'm sorry. It's just... I just... well, I didn't expect... I mean, I thought we were gonna be alone... just you and me and... long walks on the beach... splashing in the sea... I mean, you made it sound so romantic, and I was really looking forward to it.

HARRY: We will be alone. All alone, I promise. Maybe I could have a word with the girls and tell them we need a few days by ourselves.

KIMBERLY (pulling back): A few days?

HARRY: A week then. Two weeks, if you want, but right now I just need to finish these pages, okay? I promise we'll get some alone time as soon as I'm finished.

>He kisses her on the forehead and gives her the phone back. Kimberly slumps dejectedly in a chair. He grabs his papers from the table and heads for the stairs, ruffling

her hair as he passes her. Kimberly hits "speed dial" on her cell.

KIMBERLY: Hi Mom, it's me. Have you ever heard of an old movie called "When Harry Met Sally?"

Lights dim.

Scene 3

> Lights come up. We're on the sundeck where Gloria, Abby, Jessica, and Kimberly are sitting on sun loungers. Gloria is rubbing suntan lotion into her arms, Abby is reading a book, and Jessica and Kimberly are relaxing in the sun.

GLORIA: So Kimberly, how are you enjoying your day at the Playboy Mansion?

KIMBERLY: My what?

GLORIA: (motions around her) Your day at the Playboy Mansion, with Hugh "Harry" Heffner and us Playboy Bunnies.

ABBY: (looking up from her book) Playboy Bunnies? I'm way too intelligent to be a bunny... and you're way too old!

> Jessica laughs as Gloria throws a towel at Abby.

GLORIA: Fuck you, Abby. Okay, forget the Playboy Mansion. How are you enjoying your day here with us in the house?

KIMBERLY: It's okay. The view's nice.

> She looks dreamily towards the ocean.

GLORIA: Yeah, but it must feel just a little odd, spending so much time with three old bags like us. Especially since we were all married to your man at one time or another.

KIMBERLY: (shrugs) Well, I knew Harry had a life before he met me—

JESSICA (wry smile): But you didn't expect it to be still going on in the form of three ex-wives, right? I mean, how could you? I sure as hell wouldn't.

KIMBERLY: Yet you put up with it? Why was that?

JESSICA: Good question. (reflects) I loved him I guess is the only answer.

GLORIA: Ugh, I may just barf.

JESSICA (to Gloria): That doesn't mean I didn't wish all of you would disappear. I did. (to Kimberly) But after a while I... oh, I don't know, I suppose I got used to having them over, you know, like relatives. (nods towards Gloria) Older relatives of course.

GLORIA: By older relatives I take it you mean Lila.

KIMBERLY: Lila? Who's Lila?

ABBY (lowers her book): Harry's first wife. She got remarried to a big shot lawyer named Drake Harrington and has managed to survive rather nicely without Harry, much to his dismay.

KIMBERLY (getting agitated): Another one? Jesus, how many more of you are there? And no offense to you, but why the hell does he need his ex-wives hanging around him all the time?

ABBY: I wish I knew.

KIMBERLY: It's like an episode from *Big Love*! Except they're all still married and—

ABBY: Mattie told Harry the same thing. Says he's got a harem complex. Told him to move to Utah where it's legal to have more than one wife then he wouldn't have to bother getting divorced—

JESSICA: It's not legal in Utah. Not anymore. Other than if you live in one of those compounds.

ABBY (ignoring Jessica): Which—and you won't believe this— actually offended Harry. Seems down deep, our boy has a Puritan streak.

GLORIA: Well, I for one wish I'd put a stop to it while I had the chance. If I'd stopped him having contact with Lila after we'd hooked up, we'd probably still be together today. (to Kimberly) If I were you, I'd have a talk to Harry because if he's truly serious about you, there ain't no reason at all why he needs to spend so much time with us.

JESSICA (playing along): Oh I agree. Put your foot down. Show him who's boss. He'll love you all the more for it. Don't you agree Abby?

ABBY: Absolutely.

> Abby, Gloria, and Jessica busy themselves with their books and suntan oil, leaving Kimberly deep in thought. Suddenly, she gets up and nods her head.

KIMBERLY: You're right. Hanging out with the ex-wives obviously didn't work for you guys. If this is going to work for me, then I need to put my foot down right now. Wish me luck!

ABBY/JESSICA/GLORIA (faking enthusiasm): Good luck!!

> Kimberly innocently skips off into the house.

ABBY: Well, I guess that takes care of that.

JESSICA: Poor kid. She'll be out of here before sunset.

GLORIA: And not a moment too soon.

> Lights dim.

Scene 4

> Lights come up. We're in the living room. Harry works at his computer, while Kimberly stands nearby, pouting.

KIMBERLY: All I want, Harry—all any girl would want—is for you to stop seeing them altogether.

HARRY (looks up, surprised): Altogether? You mean, like, forever?

KIMBERLY: Why not?

HARRY (never occurred to him): But they're my buds.

KIMBERLY: No, no, they're your <u>ex-wives</u>.

HARRY: So?

KIMBERLY: So ex-wives and ex-husbands cannot be buddies.

HARRY: Oh shit, not this again. Look just because you can't be married to someone doesn't mean you have to hate them or not want 'em around.

KIMBERLY (like he's crazy): You're really serious, aren't you? Okay, maybe you don't have to hate them, but you can't still want them around, 'cause if you do then you shouldn't have divorced them in the first place—you should've tried to work things out.

HARRY: We did. We tried really hard. All of us. But some people just aren't meant to live together. That still doesn't mean we don't care about each other or want to hang out together—

KIMBERLY: It does if you want to get on with your life—be with someone else. (off his frown) You do want to be with me, Harry, right?"

HARRY: More than anything.

KIMBERLY: Good. 'Cause I feel the same way. (kisses him) I love you, Harry. And I want to be with you. But I want to be with you alone. Not sharing you with a bunch of has-beens who, nice as they are, should just get on with their own lives. (softening) Will you do that for me, Harry? Will you tell your exes they can't come around anymore—in your own sweet way, of course.

HARRY (trapped): I... uh... when?

KIMBERLY: Well, if you're serious about us, it has to be as soon as possible, Harry. Like, right now.

HARRY: Erm, I guess I could ask if—

KIMBERLEY (before he can say any more): Excellent, that's settled then. Okay, I'm going up to take a quick shower. See you in five.

> She runs off upstairs. Harry looks after her, unable to believe what he just agreed to. Then a faint NOISE behind the kitchen door makes him scowl.

HARRY: You can come out now, Mattie.

> The door inches open, revealing Mattie, who's obviously been listening. The two eyeball each other then:

MATTIE: Looks like you cooked yourself this time, Harry.

HARRY: You don't have to be so goddamn happy about it.

MATTIE: I'm not happy or sad. But if you want my opinion—

HARRY: I don't.

MATTIE: Well, you're getting it anyway. I think it's for the best. For everyone involved.

She returns to the kitchen, leaving Harry standing there like a dog that's lost its favorite bone.

Lights dim.

Scene 5

Living room. Harry is talking on his cell phone while drinking a scotch-on-the-rocks.

HARRY: Look, I know you're in a hurry to get the new pages but some of the changes don't make sense... What? Which ones? Well, for openers, if I omit scenes fifty-seven through fifty-nine, like you suggested, it will mean Hank has spent the last five minutes talking to his horse instead of... (pause) I said his HORSE... that's right—instead of his girlfriend Claire; and though I know you want this to be a contemporary western, and lately cowboys have been having affairs with some rather "unique" partners, I don't believe you want your quiet-man-of-integrity to be in love with his fucking horse! (long pause while Harry listens to the person on the phone) No, I didn't ask her about Nick Cage yet. (listens) Yes, I agree that he'd be great for the part, but I'm not going to push it. (listens) Why not? Well, for starters, because I don't want her to think I'm some kind of dubious prick who's only with her because of her uncle, that's why. (listens) No, that's not the reason I'm with her. (listens) No, no, I'm with her because she's a great girl. (listens) What? That's not true. Look, just because she's a hottie doesn't mean she can't also be great. (listens) That's right. No other reason I'm with her, other than love. Right—

The exterior door opens and in walks Gloria. She hesitates as she sees Harry on the phone, but he waves her in.

HARRY (into the phone): I've got to go. Just do me a favor and decide exactly what changes you want and e-mail them over tonight. Otherwise you can find some other schmuck to work on this godforsaken script while I get back to topping up my tan. (He hangs up)

GLORIA: You do realize, don't you, that he probably will get someone else to work on that godforsaken script after the way you just spoke to him.

HARRY (sighs): I know, I know. I just got stuff on my mind, that's all.

GLORIA (feigning innocence): Why, what's happened?

HARRY: Look, I'm not going to lie. It's Kimberly. She wants me to stop seeing you guys.

GLORIA (shocked): What? Well, fuck her! What makes that little bitch think you'll drop us just because she says so. Jesus, Harry, what did she say when you put her in her place? Was she shocked?

　　Harry shifts uncomfortably and avoids her glare.

GLORIA: Har-ry, you did, didn't you? (his silence says "no" and she sighs) Exactly what did you say to her?

HARRY: I... uhm... sort of promised her that I'd ask you all to buzz off.

GLORIA: You did what?

HARRY: Look, I love you guys, you know I do, but Kimberly... she's like a breath of fresh air. I really like her; she's a great girl.

GLORIA (in surprise): She is? I mean, she is!

HARRY: Yeah, she's beautiful, she's caring, and she can do things in the sack that no other woman has ever done before. (he leans in closer) Y'know, she does this one thing where she gets her finger and...

GLORIA (furious): Okay, okay, stop! I don't need to hear this. (she screws up her face in horror) Look, I know it's none of my business, and it probably isn't my place to say, but are you sure about her? I mean, is it possible that maybe you're just with her because of her connections?

HARRY: Her connections? Oh, you mean Nick Cage? (exasperated) Why do people keep saying that? Do you all really think I'm that shallow?

GLORIA: Well, you've got to admit that having an international star in the family would be a great boost for your career.

HARRY: Maybe.

GLORIA: *Maybe*?!

HARRY: Okay, okay, it would be a boost, I admit that. It just hadn't occurred to me, that's all.

GLORIA: Really? Well, it's occurred to everyone else!

> Harry slumps down in a chair, questioning himself and talking to no one in particular.

HARRY: Jesus, am I really capable of that? Of liking someone purely because of someone they know? (beat) Maybe I am. Maybe subconsciously I like the idea of writing something for a megastar: someone with real talent who can finally get me away from writing crappy soaps all day.

GLORIA: Now you're talking.

HARRY (not listening; continues to speak to himself): Could that be the real reason why I like her? (long beat) If it is, I've got some serious soul-searching to do. Maybe I just gotta admit I really am a shallow schmuck after all, and just get it over with.

GLORIA: No way! I couldn't have loved you if you were, and neither could Abby or Jessica. Well, maybe Jessica, but... (trying to change the subject) Look, forget I said anything, okay? I'm sure you do genuinely like her. Maybe even (nearly chokes on her words) love her. It was stupid of me to bring it up. I'm sorry.

HARRY: Hey, you've spent time with her today. What do you think of her?

GLORIA (hesitantly): Well, she's... uhm... she's... different.

HARRY (brightens): Isn't she though? Yeah, she's great, really great. So much energy too.

GLORIA: That's 'cause she's just out of puberty, Harry.

Harry shoots her a look, and she quickly changes track.

GLORIA: Well, she definitely seems very "special," I'll give her that.

HARRY (suddenly interested): Special? In what way special?

GLORIA (struggling to think of something): Well, she's very... She's very... flexible.

HARRY: Flexible. Yeah, she is. What else?

GLORIA: Uhm, she's healthy. Definitely healthy.

HARRY: Go on.

GLORIA: Well, she's... she's... she's got nice hair. And tits: her tits are quite—

HARRY: Quite what?

GLORIA: Perky?

HARRY: Man, you can say that again! Y'know Gloria, I didn't know whether to do this or not, but after speaking with you I'm pretty sure...

GLORIA (confused): Sure of what?

HARRY: I'm gonna ask Kimberly to marry me.

GLORIA: You're what? Are you fucking nuts? You've only known her for a heartbeat.

HARRY: Yeah, but when you make up your mind about something, there's no point in waiting around.

>   He jumps up out of the chair, very excited.

GLORIA: But what about Nick Cage... your soul-searching... and all that other shit?

HARRY (waving her comments aside): Aww forget it. Who cares? I know what I want. And you made me realize just how very special she is. (he kisses her on the head) Thanks Glo-Worm, I owe you one.

>   He walks toward the stairs just as the sundeck door opens and Abby and Jessica enter.

GLORIA: But I didn't do anything!!!

HARRY (re: his ex-wives) I'll leave you to tell 'em the good news.

ABBY: What good news?

JESSICA: What's going on?

GLORIA: We've been royally fucked. That's what's going on.

>   Abby and Jessica look at Gloria, concerned, then look at the stairs, where Harry has just disappeared.

>   Lights dim.

Scene 6

The lights come up to reveal Abby, Gloria, and Jessica sitting in the living room, while Mattie stands in front of them, placing mugs of coffee onto the table from a tray.

MATTIE: Well, if you want my advice—

GLORIA: We don't.

MATTIE (continuing anyway): You're not gonna like this, but the time has come for you all to move on. Kimberly seems like a great gal, so if you really want Harry to be happy, you'll quit hanging around and let him get on with his life. If he's ready to settle down, then you should all just wish him luck. No use living in each other's pockets all the time—that won't do anyone any good.

> She tucks the tray under her arm and goes into the kitchen.

ABBY: She has a point, you know. How can you get on with your life if you're well and truly anchored in the past?

GLORIA: Oh, what the hell does she know? The nearest Mattie ever got to marriage was a crush on her second cousin when she was fourteen.

JESSICA: I hate to admit it, but I think she's right. I mean I'm supposed to be marrying Richard in just over a month, and look at me! I spend every weekend with my ex-husband and his ex-wives! It's probably not the most sensible thing to do, is it? And look at Abby; she doesn't know if she's coming or going with Brett, and that's all because of Harry.

ABBY (surprised): How'd you figure that out?

JESSICA: Think about it. If Harry was out of the picture, you wouldn't be hanging round here every Saturday afternoon.

Instead you'd be out with Brett, picking out placemats for your new house.

GLORIA: You're moving in together?

ABBY: Only in Jessica's head.

JESSICA: And then there's Gloria.

GLORIA: What about Gloria?

JESSICA: If you could kiss Harry goodbye, then perhaps you could finally get yourself a new man. After all, you haven't been with anyone since you divorced him, and that's just not normal.

GLORIA (irked): Excuse me. Just 'cause I don't share every detail of my life with you doesn't mean I haven't had anyone, thank you very much. And if you spent more time worrying about your own relationship, and less time thinking about other people's, then perhaps you'd finally make up your mind about Richard and stop boring the rest of us with tales about him.

JESSICA: Hey, that's not fair! I don't bore anyone with tales about Richard. In fact if anyone's boring anyone around here, it's you with your sarcasm and menopausal mood swings.

GLORIA: Menopausal mood swings? Are you fucking kidding me?

> They're about to attack each other when Abby, ever the sensible one of the trio, steps between them.

ABBY: Will you two grow up? Look, it doesn't matter how much time we do or don't spend with Harry. The important thing is that we don't want him to end up with that dim-witted little Popsicle, and we need to find a way of stopping it. Agreed?

JESSICA: Agreed.

ABBY: Gloria?

GLORIA: Yes, agreed. But how are we gonna do it? We already tried and it just made everything a hundred times worse. He's too hooked on her to listen to us.

ABBY: Maybe, maybe not. (thinks) Listen, what do we actually know about Kimberly? She's a fitness instructor and her uncle is Nick Cage, that's it. There must be something in her past that could trip her up.

JESSICA: Possibly. But how could we find out?

GLORIA: We're women, aren't we? We can find out anything.

ABBY (going to the computer): That's true, and as women we are certainly good, but Google is better. Come on, we've got some research to do.

    Gloria and Jessica swap "what can we lose?" looks, and they follow her. Abby begins tapping away on the keys.

JESSICA: If Harry catches you on his computer, he'll freak. He already went ballistic just because I looked at his papers.

GLORIA: Don't tell him then! Why don't you do something useful—keep a lookout, make sure he doesn't come down here.

    Jessica shrugs and hurries to the foot of the stairs.

GLORIA (to Abby): Come on, come on, hurry up.

ABBY: I'm hurrying. (typing) Oh shit, Kimberly Woods brings up 18,800,000 pages.

GLORIA: Can't you do some kind of advanced search? Try Dimwit Kimberly Woods, that'll bring her up.

ABBY: Hey! Here's one. (reading from the site) "Official website of Kimberly Woods, masseuse and aerobics instructor". That's got to be her.

She clicks on the site. Gloria leans down in anticipation. Jessica rejoins them, anxious to see what's happening.

ABBY (reading from site): "Kimberly Woods is an aerobics instructor, massage therapist, and artist."

GLORIA: Con artist, more like.

ABBY (continues to read): "She was born in Idaho and moved to California to become a fitness instructor to the stars."

GLORIA: Christ, this is the most boring site I've ever seen.

JESSICA (shouting from the stairs): That's 'cause all you look at is porn.

GLORIA: Fuck off.

ABBY: Hey, look at this. It's a guestbook.

GLORIA: Guestbook? Who the hell would want to sign that?

ABBY: Hopefully someone who can lead us to some dirt. (she presses a key, but nothing happens) Shit!

GLORIA: What's wrong? Go into it, for Christ's sake.

ABBY: I can't, its password protected. I can't get into it at all.

She continues to type, trying various words.

GLORIA: Password protected? Why would you block a website?

JESSICA (from the stairs): Probably to detract spammers.

GLORIA (rolling her eyes): Spammers?

JESSICA: Spammers. People who send junk emails about Viagra and sex toys and stuff.

GLORIA: I know what spammers are, you idiot. What I'm wondering is why anyone would want to spam this shitty little site.

> Jessica leaves her post by the stairs and wanders over to educate the others.

JESSICA: Spammers don't really care how boring a site is, they just target anything they can find, usually through search engines and—

GLORIA: Jessica! Enough of your crap! Just shut up for two minutes, okay?

ABBY: I wish you'd both shut up. You're driving me nuts.

GLORIA (to Jessica): I thought you were keeping a lookout for Harry?

JESSICA: I am, I am.

> Pissed, she goes back to the stairs. But instead of looking for Harry, she takes an iPad from her purse, which is hanging over the banister. She types away, not noticed by the others.

ABBY (frustrated): Hopeless! I can't get into it, no matter what password I try.

GLORIA: What about "hot buns"?

ABBY: Hot buns?

GLORIA: Worth a shot at least.

> Abby types "hot buns" into the computer and shakes her head.

ABBY: Nope.

GLORIA: Hottie?

Abby types the word into the computer.

ABBY: Uh-uh.

GLORIA: Blow job?

ABBY: Gloria!

GLORIA: Just try it.

ABBY (she sighs but does it): Uh-uh.

GLORIA: Big jugs.

ABBY (rolls her eyes; types): Nada. (types) "Legs" doesn't work either. Shit. I was sure this was going to work.

GLORIA: So was I. Fuck. We're obviously losing our touch.

JESSICA (from the stairs): Speak for yourself.

> Gloria and Abby both look toward Jessica as she waves her iPad at them, smiling wildly.

ABBY: What?

GLORIA: Stop smirking and tell us.

JESSICA: Nick Cage's Facebook page.

ABBY: Facebook page? How'd you find that?

JESSICA (joins them with her iPad): Simple. I just searched for Kimberly, then I viewed her friends list. She might be bright enough to protect herself with passwords, but seems Uncle Nick isn't so smart: he's got his profile listed as public, so I just got through straight away.

ABBY: Way to go, Jessica!

Jessica shrugs, as if she does this type of stuff every day.

GLORIA: Well, well, well, seems you might have a brain after all.

Jessica pulls a face at Gloria and hands Abby the iPad. Abby checks the screen.

ABBY (reads): "Welcome to the official profile of Nick Cage; Idaho's most prolific pig farmer." (to the others, confused) Pig farmer?

All three study the page intently. Then they look at each other and suddenly burst out laughing.

GLORIA: Oh, this is great. Not only is he not THE Nicolas Cage, he's a fucking pig farmer? (laughs) Jesus! The closest Harry'll get to working with him is a trip to the abattoir. (pause as they all look at the screen) Here, give it to me.

Gloria takes the iPad from Abby and starts typing.

JESSICA: What're you doing?

GLORIA: I'm sending a screenshot of this to the printer. It's way too good to keep to ourselves.

The printer whirrs into action. Just then, Kimberly comes running down the stairs, shouting to them.

KIMBERLY: Guys, guys, guess what?

The women turn abruptly. Gloria grabs the page from the printer and gives it to Jessica, who quickly hands it to Abby. Then Jessica grabs the iPad from Gloria and stuffs it back into her handbag.

ABBY/GLORIA/JESSICA: What's up?

Kimberly sees something suspicious is going on, but continues, regardless.

KIMBERLY: Harry just asked me to marry him! Isn't that fabuloso?

ABBY: Fabuloso.

JESSICA: Marvelous.

GLORIA: Divine.

> Abby tries to hide the page behind her back, but Kimberly sees what she's doing.

KIMBERLY: What're you hiding?

ABBY/GLORIA/JESSICA: Nothing.

KIMBERLY (suspicious): Please tell me. If you're hiding something from me, I'd really like to know what it is.

> Abby looks at Gloria and Jessica, and both nod soberly. Abby hands the page to Kimberly. She examines it briefly then looks at Abby, confused.

KIMBERLY: Where'd you get this?

ABBY: From Jessica.

JESSICA: I got it from Gloria.

GLORIA: Jessica got it from her iPad. (pause) It's your uncle's Facebook profile.

KIMBERLY: I know what it is. But why are you looking at it? I don't understand.

GLORIA: That makes four of us.

KIMBERLY: What do you mean?

GLORIA: Well, what we don't understand is why you would tell Harry that your uncle is Nick Cage—as-in movie-star-Nicolas-Cage—when all the time he was Nick Cage the pig farmer!

KIMBERLY: I.... I.....

> Just then Mattie enters. She grabs the paper, crumples it up, and throws it onto the desk. She hugs Kimberly in a motherly embrace. Kimberly begins to sob.

MATTIE: There, there, don't worry. Mattie's here. Shh.... (she looks at the ex-wives): You should be ashamed of yourselves. All of you.

> Harry now gallops down the stairs. He sees Mattie holding Kimberly and grins, unaware that she's upset.

HARRY: I see she's told you the good news!

ABBY: You could say that.

HARRY: Emotional little thing: started crying when I asked her to marry me, too. (takes Kimberly from Mattie and cuddles her) Come on, baby, cheer up. This is a proposal, not a funeral.

GLORIA (picks up the crumpled paper): Maybe you should look at—

> She breaks off as the front door suddenly flies open. They all turn to the door, startled, as a smartly dressed woman enters.

MATTIE (alarmed): Uh-oh. Now the shit's really gonna hit the fan.

> She ducks into the kitchen. The woman, a chic blonde in her forties, is Harry's first wife, LILA. Though American, she SPEAKS with a FAKE BRITISH ACCENT. She stares down her nose at Harry as if she's slumming just by talking to him. She then gives the other women a dismissive look.

LILA: Good afternoon, Harry. (taking off her hat and coat and looking around for someone to hand them to) Where's Mattie?

   Mattie rushes in from the kitchen.

MATTIE: Here I am Lila. Let me take those for you.

   She takes Lila's hat and coat, and she returns to the kitchen.

HARRY: Lila, what are you doing here?

LILA: I was driving by and I thought I'd pop in to see how you are.

   Abby, Gloria, and Jessica swap looks: "Pop in"?!

Silly me, I thought maybe you were lonely, sitting here all by yourself on a Saturday evening. But I should have known better.

GLORIA: The only time Harry's been lonely was while he was married to you, Lila. I think it was the separate bedrooms that did it.

   Lila shoots Gloria a look, then turns to Abby and Jessica.

LILA (gives them her signature phony "air kiss"): Abby! Jessica! How are you? Haven't seen you in ages. How are things going? Still busy-busy? (before they can reply, she looks at Kimberly) Harry, you never told me you had a daughter.

KIMBERLY: I'm Harry's fiancée.

   Lila looks down her nose at Kimberly and fakes enthusiasm.

LILA: Oh, how simply marvelous. Let me see your ring. (she lifts Kimberly's hand, grimaces when she sees no ring) Oh, you poor child! (to Harry) Don't tell me your endless supply of rings has finally run out? (to Gloria) Why don't you give her your old one? After all the weight you've gained recently, I'm quite sure it doesn't fit you anymore.

> Gloria dives for Lila, but is held back by Abby.

HARRY: Lila, why are you really here?

LILA: I have good news.

ABBY (aside to Jessica): What's with the British accent?

JESSICA: I think she's turned into Nicole Kidman.

ABBY: She's Australian you dope.

> Ignoring them, Lila sits down on the chair and starts to brush away imaginary pieces of dust from its arms.

LILA: Harry, as you know, my husband and I have been spending a lot of time in London. He's working on a big case over there, and I've been… well let's just say Harrods's profits have gone up ten-fold since I arrived.

> She laughs, though no one else thinks she's funny.

Anyway… After some discussion, we've decided that rather than constantly flying back and forth, we might as well move over there. We've found a great place in Holland Park, and we're in the process of signing the paperwork as we speak.

HARRY: That's great, Lila. But what's that got to do with me?

LILA: Harry darling, it's like this. If I'm going to move to London, I need some serious cash to spend. There are just too many fantastic stores over there, and you know what Drake is like. He may be a good husband, but he's even better at keeping his wallet shut.

GLORIA (aside): Just like your legs.

LILA (shoots Gloria a loathsome look): Long story short, I've decided to sell this house.

HARRY: What?! B-But you love this house.

LILA: Yes. But it has far more bad memories than good, I'm afraid. (gives Gloria another look) Besides, it's not like I'm selling it to a stranger.

HARRY: You're not?

LILA: No. I'm delighted to say that Mattie has decided to buy it from me.

ABBY/GLORIA/JESSICA/HARRY (in chorus): MATTIE???

   Mattie appears with a tape measure in her hand.

MATTIE: Did I forget to tell you? Yes, that's right ladies and gents, I'm the new owner of this little beach shack. Me and Lila have been talking about it for the past two months. (beat) So Harry, much as I hate to do it, I'm gonna have to throw you out. (she scowls at the women) That goes for your harem too.

HARRY: Mattie, how the hell can you afford a place like this?

MATTIE: Honey, that's simple. I ain't ever been married.

JESSICA: Lots of people have never been married, Mattie, and they still can't afford to live in Malibu.

MATTIE: Maybe they don't know how to save money like I do. (she goes to the window and starts measuring the curtains) Perhaps if you'd ever listened to my advice, Harry—stopped playing musical beds with your wives and blowing all your money on hotties—then you could afford a place of your own too.

   Everyone looks at Mattie in shock, especially Kimberly.

KIMBERLY (to Harry): Whoa, whoa... I don't understand. What does she mean, she's selling the house? I thought it was your house?

Before he can answer, Lila laughs.

LILA: Oh, good God, no! Harry couldn't afford to live in a dumpster when he married me. This has always been my house my dear. Harry just pays rent like any other tenant would.

KIMBERLY (to Harry): You lied to me!

HARRY: About what?

KIMBERLY: You told me this was your house.

HARRY: No, I didn't. You asked where I lived and I said Malibu.

KIMBERLY: Yes, and I thought—

HARRY: That I was rich? Sorry, I'm not. (to his ex-wives) Did I ever tell you this was my house?

They each shake their head.

KIMBERLY: Okay, maybe you never said it was yours but you sure as hell never said it wasn't.

HARRY: Maybe I didn't think it mattered. (looks at her intently) Does it matter?

Kimberly hesitates...

GLORIA: Uh-oh. Trouble in paradise.

JESSICA: It looks like you both assumed too much.

HARRY: What do you mean?

JESSICA (to Abby): Show him the website.

HARRY: What website?

> Abby hands Harry the crumpled printout of the Nick Cage pig farmer profile.

GLORIA: Seems that Miss Hard Buns has been keeping things from you too.

> Harry straightens out the paper, scans it, and looks at Kimberly, who avoids his gaze.

HARRY: Your uncle is Nick Cage, a pig farmer from Idaho?

JESSICA: Surprise, surprise!

> Harry starts laughing. Big belly laughs.

ABBY: What's so funny? We thought you'd be really pissed.

HARRY: No way. Don't you see, this is great news. Now I know for sure I'm not in love with Kimberly just because of her famous uncle. I love her because of her! It's the best thing that could've possibly happened!

ABBY: It is?

HARRY: Absolutely.

GLORIA: Congratulations, Harry, you do have hidden depths after all.

HARRY: Yeah, I even surprise myself sometimes.

KIMBERLY: So you still want to marry me, even though I lied to you?

HARRY: Of course! (beat) You still want to marry me, don't you? Even though I'm not rich and don't own a beach house?

KIMBERLY: N-No, I mean yes, I... I... I'm just a bit shocked that's all.

HARRY: Shocked?

KIMBERLY: Look, don't get me wrong. I still love you and all that, but it's just....

HARRY: Just what?

GLORIA: She just means that she loved you a whole lot more when you had money, right, sweetie?

> Kimberly shrugs in a matter-of-fact way, while Harry looks as though he's seeing her for the very first time.

HARRY: Oh.

> They stand in silent discomfort while the ex-wives look on. Gloria picks up a glass from the table and holds it up in toast.

GLORIA: Don't you just love happy endings? Cheers!

> Gloria drinks while the "happy couple" strain to smile.

> Lights dim.

Scene 7

> Lights come up. We're in the forensics lab. Abby studies a slide under her scope and makes notes.
>
> Behind her, the door quietly opens. Harry enters. He looks glum, and his neatly trimmed salt-and-pepper beard indicates time has passed. He carries a potted prickly pear cactus.

ABBY (not looking up): Be with you in a sec.

HARRY: No hurry.

> At the sound of his voice, Abby whirls around, surprised.

ABBY: H-Harry...

> Harry doesn't respond. Instead, he walks to the cabinet and sets the cactus among the other pots. Abby watches him intently... a million questions burning inside her.

HARRY: Your garden's coming along great.

ABBY: Cactuses are hard to kill—kinda like ex-husbands.

HARRY: Ouch! (casually) How's Mr. Architect?

ABBY: Brett's fine, thank you—last I heard.

HARRY (perks up): You mean you guys are no longer an item?

ABBY: We never were an item, Harry—except in his mind. What're you doing here, anyway?

HARRY: I was driving by and... uh... hoped you'd have lunch with me. (re: wall clock) It's only twelve thirty. Little early for dinner, though we could make a day of it and drive up to Paradise Cove and—

ABBY: Sorry. I've got stuff to do.

HARRY: Oh come on, it's been ages since I've seen you guys. I miss you. How're you all doing anyway?

ABBY: We're busy. We've all got our own lives to lead, believe it or not.

HARRY: Too busy to spend time with old Harry?

ABBY: I know it must be a shock, but it had to happen sooner or later. We all knew Jessica was going to get married eventually, and now that Gloria's been made partner she's working seventy hour weeks. Everything's changed.

HARRY: Not you though. You're still the same.

ABBY: I wouldn't count on it. (beat) Won't Kimberly be wondering where you are?

HARRY: I doubt it. She's too involved with her new producer boyfriend to notice I'm gone.

ABBY: Now why doesn't that surprise me?

HARRY: Yeah, well I know she said it didn't matter that I wasn't rich, but guess what? It did. Seems it maybe wasn't true love after all.

    Abby absorbs his words without any trace of emotion.

ABBY: What a shock. (beat) So who's taken her place?

HARRY: No one.

ABBY: My God, really? This must be the longest you've ever been without a girlfriend, isn't it?

    Harry's only answer is to sigh heavily.

ABBY: Don't be too depressed. I'd say that's a good sign.

HARRY: If you don't mind being lonely. (beat) Even you must get lonely sometimes. Do you?

ABBY: Harry...

HARRY: I know, I know, you're busy and you want me to leave.

> He takes a business card from his pocket, hands it to her.

HARRY: Here's my new address. It's nothing fancy but at least it's mine. Well, mine and the bank's, anyway.

> Abby looks at the card.

ABBY: Tarzana. Nice neighborhood.

HARRY: It's a fixer-upper. But it has potential.

ABBY (smiles): Kind of like a writer I once knew, huh?

HARRY: It has a pool, at least. And you're welcome to use it any time.

> Abby doesn't answer. Instead, she watches him walk to the door. On reaching it, he looks back at her.

HARRY: I do miss you, y'know. (he waits but she doesn't respond) I know it's not gonna change anything, but I want to tell you anyway: letting you go was the worst mistake I ever made. (he again waits for a response—again she's silent) Anyway, I know I have a funny way of showing it, but I think deep down you know how I feel about you. So if you ever need anything—anything at all—just call me.

> He leaves. Abby looks at the business card and then at the door, mind churning. A long beat.

ABBY: Harry, wait!

    Harry comes back into the room.

This pool of yours… is it heated?

HARRY: Sometimes.

ABBY: Sometimes?

HARRY: When the heater's working. But, hey, it has a great view of the Valley.

ABBY: In that case, maybe it's worth a look.

HARRY: Oh, it's well worth that. Maybe even two looks.

    They both smile at each other.

ABBY: Tomorrow's Saturday, right?

HARRY: You betcha.

ABBY: (with fond warmth): See you around noon.

HARRY: Noon it is.

    He starts out the door and Abby looks down at her scope.

ABBY: And Harry….

HARRY: Don't worry. It'll just be you and me, babe. See ya…

    He walks out WHISTLING "Sunny side of the street."

    Abby looks after him and shakes her head fondly.

ABBY (to herself): The more things change, the more they stay the same.

Walking to the cabinet, she puts Harry's latest cactus in the center in the front row of pots...

Lights dim. Final Curtain.

The End

www.ingramcontent.com/pod-product-compliance
Lightning Source LLC
Chambersburg PA
CBHW071459160426
43195CB00013B/2155